THE
TRUTH
THAT
TRANSFORMED
ME

THE LIFE OF D. JAMES KENNEDY

'Turn on the television almost anywhere in America and in many places all over the world and there he is, Dr. D. James Kennedy. Open a magazine and there is an article by Dr. Kennedy. Visit on the right day in the nation's Capitol and he is there. In thousands of churches Evangelism Explosion, his unique approach to gospel witness, is currently or has been in the recent past employed. Who is this remarkable man? For the benefit of those who do not know him well, *The Truth that Transformed Me: The Life of D. James Kennedy*, is the remarkable account of one of the most beloved preachers of the late twentieth and early twenty-first century. This biography will both challenge the reader and inspire him in his own devotional walk with Christ.'

Paige Patterson, President,
Southwestern Baptist Theological Seminary, Fort Worth, Texas

'It is an unassailable fact that Dr. D. James Kennedy through the ministry of Evangelism Explosion has done as much or more than any individual in the last 40 to 50 years to, not only promote evangelism but, provide an avenue to train every day Christians to participate in the joy of leading men and women to Christ. From the first time I read his quote, "Evangelism is more caught than taught" it has encouraged and stimulated, not only me but, countless thousands around the world. Men of God whom the Lord uses can seem distant however this book allows you, in an inviting way, to meet and get to know "Jimmy" Kennedy. Read it...You are about to get a new best friend.'

Harry L. Reeder, Senior Pastor
Briarwood Presbyterian Church, Birmingham, Alabama

'More than anybody I know, Dr. D. James Kennedy epitomizes evangelism and the sovereignty of God in his ministry. His influence on me has been profound. This well-written biography provides a history, wonderful anecdotes and insights into one of America's most powerful Christian leaders of our generation.'

R T Kendall

THE
TRUTH
THAT
TRANSFORMED
ME

THE LIFE OF D. JAMES KENNEDY

Mary Lou Davis

CHRISTIAN FOCUS

© D. James Kennedy

ISBN 1-84550-206-X
ISBN 978-1-84550-206-5

10 9 8 7 6 5 4 3 2 1

Published in 2006
by
Christian Focus Publications Ltd.,
Geanies House, Fearn, Tain,
Ross-shire, IV20 1TW, Great Britain
www.christianfocus.com

Cover design by Danie Van Straaten

Printed and bound by WS Bookwell, Finland

Contents

1

WHY AM I HERE?

At 3:15 p.m. Jimmy Kennedy sprinted down the sidewalk. He inhaled deeply as if he had held his breath all day unwilling to taint his lungs with schoolroom air. Eight in the morning to three in the afternoon is an eternity for any thirteen-year-old and Jimmy looked forward to the comfort of home.

The heavy door of his apartment building slammed behind him as he ran toward the staircase. Just as he began to climb, a loud *whump* shook the building causing the overhead light to dance on its long chain. The light made weird shadows as it slowly swung back and forth. Jimmy froze and listened. He cocked his head in an effort to hear any other telling sound. He strained to see past the landing above him. No one had bothered to replace the burned out light in the second floor hallway. The bulb dangling in the entrance lacked the wattage to penetrate the shroud of darkness beyond it.

The hairs on the back of Jimmy's neck prickled with a faint flicker of alarm. He shook his head to clear his mind from the thoughts his imagination conjured. 'It couldn't have come from our place,' he whispered to calm his nerves. 'The thump was too loud to come from there.'

His mouth felt dry, and he swallowed hard and ran the back of his hand across his lips. The door of his apartment loomed near the top of the dark staircase, and suddenly he was afraid to enter. He approached his door on tiptoe and pressed his ear against it. Closing his eyes to shut out all distractions, he listened.

Within moments a crash of splintering glass caused him to jump back in alarm. Mumbled cursing followed the noise. He pressed his back against the wall and glanced up and down the hall to see if anyone else had heard the sound.

No one appeared. He was alone. His pulse pounded in his temples as he cautiously turned the doorknob. Unconsciously shielding himself, Jimmy clutched his books to his chest and stepped inside. The reek of booze socked him with an invisible fist. He turned around to run but stopped at the door. Over his shoulder he called, 'Mom?' in a high thin voice.

Jimmy scowled, cleared his throat and tried again in the deeper tone he acquired on his last birthday. 'Mom?'

No answer.

Jimmy glanced around. The living room was in shambles. *Had an intruder broken in*, he wondered. He slunk down the dark hall toward the kitchen, drawn toward the sound of cabinet doors and drawers being flung open and slammed. Someone must be searching for something and angry they can't find it. He gripped the doorjamb, pressed his face against his hand, and peered into the bright room. Forks, knives and spoons exploded from the cutlery drawer as it was yanked open. Jimmy shrunk back, but he had seen what he feared most. He closed his eyes and began to tremble.

'It's okay,' he whispered to himself. He took several deep breaths to calm his nerves, then squared his shoulders and stepped into the light.

'Mom, I'm home from school.'

She wheeled around and glared as if he were a stranger – an intruder. She muttered something unintelligible under her breath then turned and began searching the cupboards again.

'Where is it?' she growled. Glancing over her shoulder at Jimmy she asked, 'Have you hidden it, boy?'

'No ma'am,' he said as he inched into the kitchen.

She crunched across the broken glass that littered the floor. No liquid pooled in the shards, so he figured his mother smashed her bottle after she'd drunk it dry.

'Ah, here you are,' his mother crooned. Jimmy looked up hopefully. His mom was kind and gentle when sober. Unfortunately, her soft words were not for him. Her eyes were on the drink she craved. The deceitful beverage lured the weak with promises of bliss then betrayed them. It poisoned and robbed its lovers of their senses and replaced his mother with a monster.

She whipped around and fixed bloodshot eyes on Jimmy. 'Get out of here! Why are you home? Get out! Get out!'

Jimmy dropped his shield. The schoolbooks he clutched tumbled to the floor. They had no real power to protect him. Pierced by words, he ran.

The chill wind that blew off Lake Michigan washed from Jimmy's memory the smell of alcohol that saturated the apartment. He opened his mouth and sucked in deeply as he fled the few blocks toward the beach. Dark waves lapped the shore and their constant beating lulled his heart and slowed its pace. Jimmy threw himself on the sand, breathing hard and cursing the asthma his father genetically gifted him.

America had entered the war in December when the Japanese bombed Pearl Harbor. But Jimmy's personal battles seemed a lot closer to home than those in Europe and Asia.

'I wish mother wouldn't drink!' he whispered to the fathomless blue sky that stretched above him. As he stared up, gravity drew tears down from the corners of his eyes across his temples. The thudding of his heart slowed to a regular thump, thumping. As he listened to its cadence, he imagined the pounding was the sound of the gears that churned the engines rotating the earth on its axis. His fingers dug into the sand to grab hold and keep himself from hurtling into outer space if the rotation of the planet ground to a halt.

The heavens stretched in an endless sea of blue, wider and deeper than the great lake that lapped the shore beside him. 'I know you're up there, God,' he said to the expanse. 'I know you've got to have more for me than this.' He threw a handful of sand backward in the direction of his apartment. He lay still and cupped his ear. 'I'm listening,' he whispered. 'Why am I here? Tell me what you want. I know you must have a purpose for me.'

A shadow moved over him, cooling the warmth of the sun. He shielded his eyes with a hand and looked up. Sand sprayed him in a shower of grit. Jimmy jerked up spitting. He brushed the grains from of his face and squinted at the dark form looming above.

'Your purpose is to deliver groceries,' said a large boy standing with legs wide apart and meaty fists planted on his hips. His bulk blocked out the sky. 'Get up and get going if you're gonna keep your little job.'

'You didn't have to kick sand in my face, George!' Jimmy yelled. He jumped up with fists full of the gritty ammo.

'Uh, uh, little brother.' George put his palm on Jimmy's forehead, holding the smaller boy at arm's length. Jimmy's fists punched air as he swung uselessly at his brother. 'Let me go!' he said through gritted teeth.

'Fine,' George said, abruptly jerking his hand away and stepping to the side. Jimmy stumbled forward and hit the ground on hands and knees.

'Why don't you save that energy for your grocery delivery bike. You'll need it to carry all those brown bags up the steps of Mrs. Stabler's apartment.'

'You're just jealous that I've almost got enough money to go to Boy Scout camp. While I'm camping in the woods and getting my lifeguard certificate, you'll be stuck alone in the apartment with Mom and her booze.'

'Me! Jealous of you?' George barked out a harsh laugh. A deep line furrowed his brow and his mouth twitched down on one side. 'While you're gone I'll be having a party. Dad's gonna be back and he'll take me to do loads of fun things while he's home,' George said stretching his lips back in a rigid grin.

'That's a lie!' Jimmy yelled, balling his fingers into fists. 'He told us last time he was home that the glass company promoted him to a wider area. And you know what that means. He's gonna be gone on sales trips longer than ever.'

George put his palm on Jimmy's chest and shoved him backward. 'Shut up. That's all you know. You're just a kid.'

'Am not. You're just a year older than me,' Jimmy called over his shoulder as he ran off the beach. He shook his head to clear it from the verbal battle with his brother. He wished they could just be friends, but George never seemed to want him around. Jimmy trotted into the corner grocery store and stopped in front of the man behind the counter.

'Sorry I'm late, Mr. Needleman,' he said breathing hard.

'Better save your energy for delivering groceries, young man.' His tone was gruff, but a smile softened the words.

'Yes, sir. That's what my brother said.' Jimmy jerked a thumb over his shoulder in the direction of the beach.

'I've got Mrs. Stabler's order ready.' The older man gestured at the brown bags standing at attention on the counter. 'Could you also deliver Mrs. Dunwoody's groceries before your clarinet lessons?' Mr. Needleman asked, raising bushy white brows.

'I think so,' Jimmy said, glancing at the old clock on the wall as he grabbed the sacks. He carried them to the bicycle parked in front of the store and loaded them into its basket.

School was almost out and summer waited impatiently at the edge of the month. He had worked all spring to earn enough to pay for Boy Scout camp. 'Only ten more dollars, ten more dollars, ten more dollars,' he chanted under his breath as he pedaled down the street to make his deliveries. In his mind's eye he saw the trails and trees of camp instead of streets and apartment buildings. The fresh air of wilderness braced him instead of exhaust from passing cars. He couldn't wait to get out of the big city and away from the strain of not knowing if his mom would be sober and kind or drunk and raging.

The afternoon raced by in a haze. At five o'clock Jimmy climbed the steps of the bus and paid the driver before finding a seat. With his forehead pressed against the cool glass of the window, he watched the shops and apartments of his neighborhood whisk by as the bus drove into downtown Chicago to his music lessons.

He daydreamed about the Boy Scout retreat. It was a great adventure to get out of the city and hike through dense forests and swim in the clear lake. Camp was a refuge from his troubled home, but only for a short time. Music was a different story altogether. It carried his soul beyond the bounds of earth to spiritual places he hardly understood.

It was dark when he came home from his lessons. He crept up the stairs of his apartment, quietly cracked open the door and looked in. His mother lay on the couch. He set the clarinet case on the floor and pried off his shoes with trembling fingers. The handle on the case whined when he picked it up. He stopped abruptly and shot a look at his mom. She didn't move. With a soft tread, he tiptoed across the floor and paused in front of her. With white knuckles, her hand gripped a bottle as if she feared someone might pry it away. She snored softly through her slightly parted lips.

Jimmy sighed and his shoulders sagged in relief. Mom was out for the night. Nothing woke her when she passed out. He walked into the bathroom, pushed the door closed behind him and turned the lock. The latch on his clarinet case gave a metallic clicked as he opened it. When he lifted out the glossy black instrument, he saw his reflection frowning distortedly back at him from the rounded surface. He perched on the edge of the bathtub, brought the reed to his lips, and blew. The music bounced off the tiled walls in a sad eerie echo. He smiled, closed his eyes and played on, as the moment of melody lifted his soul far above his bitter reality.

2

RUINED LIFE

'Thirty-two! Forty-four! Eighty-six!' Jimmy yelled, as he glanced left and right over the backs of his teammates. 'Hike! Hike! Hike!' The football slammed into his hand. He gripped it hard, backed up three steps, and hurled a spiral down the field to his running back.

'Touchdown! touchdown!' his teammates chanted throwing their arms up in a victory salute. They crowded together, slapping helmets and punching shoulder pads. 'Great pass, Kennedy!' the coach said, grabbing Jimmy's helmet and giving it a gentle shake. 'Now get back out there on defense and don't let the other team score!'

'Yes sir, coach,' Jimmy said puffing his chest out beneath the shoulder pads. Now that he was a freshman in high school he had achieved adult status, and as quarterback the rest of the team looked to him to lead them. With his teammates behind him, he jogged onto the field and lowered himself into a ready stance at the line of scrimmage. His tall, lean form resembled a sprinter on the blocks as he prepared to dash down the field on the kickoff.

'Tweee!' the whistle blew and the line of players barreled toward each other at top speed. Jimmy sprinted straight for the guy with the ball. The player was much bigger, but he knew he could take him down.

The fans had a bird's eye view from the stands. They watched Jimmy in his red jersey lean forward, increasing his speed. The ball carrier in yellow did the same. Like bumper cars at the state fair, red and yellow jerseys streaked toward each other. Jimmy and the other boy, virtual bighorn rams, lowered their heads and slammed into each other with a jolt that could almost be felt in the bleachers. At impact the two bounced backward then crumpled onto the green field. The brown pigskin wobbled sideways for a moment before it was scooped up by a red jersey who held it high as a trophy.

Red team celebrated. Yellow lumbered, helmets lowered and shoulder pads drooping, back to their side. Both teams huddled up for the next play, not noticing one red jersey still lying motionless.

Jimmy returned to consciousness in a tumult of grunting and shouts. 'No, Kennedy! Our goal is that way.' Jimmy glanced down. The football was in his hand. He stared at it in bewilderment. 'Wh-what –,' he stuttered.

Bam! He was down.

'Ha, ha. That'll teach you, quarterback.' Jim felt a heavy weight press down on his shoulder pads as someone used his body to push themselves up.

'Wh-what happened?' Jimmy asked.

Tweee! went the whistle, and Jimmy stared at the sideline where his coach made a 'T' with his right hand over his left.

'Time out!' a referee yelled.

'Kennedy,' the coach glared at him. 'What are you doing? Our goal is that way.' He twisted Jimmy's head around to face the opposite direction.

'Wh-what?' Jimmy asked.

'Get over there.' The coach jerked his thumb toward the bench behind him. Jimmy stumbled over and plopped next to another player who perched awkwardly on a set of crutches.

'Wh-what –,' Jimmy began.

'You keep saying that,' the other boy said. 'Don't you remember?'

Jimmy unsnapped his helmet and pulled it off. It had a wad of grass and sod ground into its side. With fingers that trembled slightly, he plucked at it. Something was wrong, but he couldn't seem to clear his mind. He reached back and massaged his neck. It hurt pretty bad. 'Wh-what happened?'

'You were out cold,' the kid volunteered. 'When you came to, the coach stuck you back in the game, but evidently you'd forgotten all the plays.'

'Wow!' Jimmy said and twisted his head back and forth to test the extent of his injury.

When he got home that evening his dad greeted him at the door.

'Dad! You're back!' Jimmy grinned then grimaced as a shooting pain shot down his back.

'Hey Bud, you're not looking so good. Come on in. I've got big news!'

'Darling,' his mother crooned and laid a cool hand on his forehead. 'Are you okay?'

'Yes, ma'am,' Jimmy said, but sat down on the couch, leaned back and blew out a deep breath.

'Your dad's got big news,' his mom said, echoing his father's words. 'We've been waiting for you to come home to tell it. George!' she called, 'Come on in. Your brother's home.'

George sauntered in and flopped down next to Jimmy.

Their dad stood in front of the family shifting his weight from one foot to the other. 'Well, the doctor has advised me, because of my asthma,' he said, and paused to clear his throat, 'to move.'

'Are we moving to a house?' George asked, sitting forward and looking excited.

'N-no. I-I mean yes. Well, you'll, we'll, we'll just have to see,' their father said with a bit of a stutter.

A week later Jim walked to his new home from his first day at a new school. He had decided to drop the 'my' at the end of his name. Jim sounded more mature than Jimmy. He kicked a rock and huffed. 'Thanks a lot, Dad. Great surprise!' He threw an arm up and said to the sky, 'Not only do we move, we move 1,000 miles away to,' his mouth twisted in a grimace of distaste, 'Tampa, Florida.' Jim shoved up his sleeves and glanced at the sun with a scowl. 'It's hot and muggy-,' he slapped at a mosquito, 'and bugs are everywhere.'

He climbed on a fence and sat, elbows on knees, head in hands. His fingers twined through his hair making it stand on end. 'Junior high,' he sneered twisting the words in his mouth as if he'd swallowed a spider. 'What kind of stupid place is this?' He threw his arms out in a wide gesture. 'Everybody knows ninth grade is high school, not junior high. At least in Chicago where everyone is civilized,' he added with a chuff of disgust.

Jimmy stalked the halls of school that day frowning at the younger kids. He sat by himself at lunch and imagined that everyone whispered about or pointed at him – the new kid. He hated it.

When he got home, he locked himself in the bathroom with his precious clarinet. He piped the scales in a loud angry march up and down from low C to high and back again.

Bang, bang, bang! 'Jimmy, come out of there right now. Quit making that racket,' his mother yelled through the door.

Jimmy cracked the door open. 'What do you want?'

'Why don't you invite some boys from school to come over and play?' she asked.

'Because I never know if you are going to be drunk and acting crazy,' Jim said, and made an effort to slam the door, but his mother blocked it with her foot.

'What?' her voice sang out an octave higher than her normal tone. 'I do not get drunk and act crazy. I may drink a little, but I never get drunk!'

'Whatever you say, Mom.' Jimmy rolled his eyes and pulled the door closed.

Late that night his dad came into his room, flipped the light on and said, 'Come on son. We've got to go.'

'Dad?' Jimmy complained in a groggy voice. 'What time is it?' He grabbed the alarm clock and squinted. '2:00 a.m. What-.' his voice broke off when he looked up and saw his dad's face covered in blood.

His dad smiled grimly. 'I'm okay, but I think we need to go check into a hotel for the rest of the night.'

'Did Mom do this?' Jimmy scowled and jerked his covers back to get up. 'Why do you put up with her, Dad?'

His father swung around and glared at him. 'Don't you say one word against your mother. I won't hear it.' He emphasized each word by shaking his index finger in Jimmy's face.

Jimmy stared out the window of the car as it rolled along the empty streets on the way to find a hotel. He leaned his forehead against the glass and remembered riding the bus in Chicago and watching the familiar buildings slide by. Everything on this Florida street looked so much smaller and inferior compared to the big city he came from. He bit his lip to keep from yelling at his dad. He clenched his fists and felt the heat rise in his face. Jimmy wanted to scream. Instead he hissed under his breath, 'I can't believe you dragged me down to this Godforsaken place. You've ruined my life.'

3

RHAPSODY IN BLUE

By the end of high school Jim Kennedy discovered that Tampa, Florida, wasn't quite as bad as he had first thought when his parents uprooted him from his beloved windy city. He traded his football helmet for a two-foot-tall hat covered in white fur. Instead of huddling with his teammates on the gridiron, he marched in front of the Plant High School band directing the music with a long black baton.

Fans packed the stadium, not only to watch the game, but also to hear the Plant Panther's band play during half-time. In Jim's senior year the football team was having a run of wins. Fans screamed, cheerleaders chanted, and the band rallied everyone with their fight song. At half-time Jim led the musicians onto the field.

It was an unusually hot night and sweat beaded on Jimmy's forehead, running in rivulets down his temples. The field lights blazed, a dozen miniature suns that illuminated the field in a bright halo. As Jim wiped his brow with his forearm his eyes flew wide. 'Oh, no,' he groaned, pinching the bridge of his nose between finger and thumb.

A pretty flute player heard his sigh and laid a gloved hand on his sleeve. 'Are you okay, Jim?' she asked sweetly.

He managed a weak smile. 'It was so hot, I took off that blasted fur-covered hat.' He raised his hands, palms up, to show they were empty. 'I must have left it in the stands.'

A low murmur rose from the crowd, but Jim didn't notice. He was captivated by the blue eyes of the pretty flautist. He smiled down at her and she looked up at him through long lashes. Then she lifted her hand to his chin and gripped it tenderly between her fingers. He sucked in deeply unsure of what she would do next. Would she kiss him here in the end zone in front of the crowd of spectators. He closed his eyes and puckered his lips but opened them in surprise when instead of a kiss she twisted his head. Everyone in the band had turned in formation, facing the same direction. They all stared at something on the field. Briefly, he wondered if the football team had made a spectacular play. But when he turned and saw what everyone stared at, his heart began to race, and the temperature seemed to rise several more degrees. His jaw dropped and he sucked in a ragged breath.

'Jimmy!' a familiar voice crowed above the buzz of the crowd. Every head swiveled round and all eyes fixed on him. A group of girls covered their mouths with their hands. He could tell by their expressions they were laughing – at him.

'Jimmy! You dumb head!'

Like the waves of the Red Sea before Moses, uniformed band members parted leaving a wide path to him. Through the rift came the one person on earth he dreaded seeing – his mother. She stumbled toward him clutching his tall drum major's hat between white-knuckled fingers.

'Do I have to follow you around, little baby, and pick up your toys? Look what you left in the stands!' she said as she waggled the hat in his face. Her venomous words slurred with the stench of alcohol.

Jim snatched his hat and turned away hoping she would retreat and no one else would notice the spectacle.

'Don't you turn your back on your own mother!' she raged and struck him violently with closed fists.

Jim wheeled and grabbed at her flailing arms. As she shouted obscenities at him, he felt flecks of spit spray his face. He wrenched her arm away savagely and began to drag her toward the only exit on the fifty-yard line. The football players hadn't left the field yet. Rooted in place, they gawked at the early half-time show.

As Jim marched his mother down the field, people no longer stifled their laughter. The whole stadium hooted, catcalled and whistled. He fixed his eyes on the open gate but felt every finger that pointed them out.

'Shut up, mother,' he hissed under his breath. 'Shut up!'

Those steps he trod across the field, pushing his mother toward the exit, seemed to take an eternity to cross. The longest yards. His face burned as if he'd been on the beach all day. He forced his feet to keep walking. His mother fought him the whole way.

When they finally reached the gate, he leaned in close enough to feel his mother's breath on his cheek. 'If you ever come back out here again, I'll kill you,' he hissed through clenched teeth.

He pivoted on his heel and stalked, head held high, back to where his band awaited him to lead them. Not once did he glance over his shoulder, but he felt every eye boring holes into his back. At each step he feared his mother would pounce on him.

As he neared the end zone, he raised his baton. The band quickly formed ranks and took a collective gasp before blowing into their instruments. He ground his teeth as he walked backward, leading them onto the field. Try as he might, Jim couldn't lose himself in the music.

Music became the only thing he lived for. He closed his eyes and remembered all the times he had practiced and played.

Music won him friends and took him places. All he wanted to do was be a band director just like Mr. Lucas, his high school teacher.

Mr. Lucas seemed to have it all together. He was always cheerful and encouraging. Every Friday he invited Jim to come to church with him, but Jim didn't have time for religion. Sunday was the day to sleep in because he'd been out late Saturday night.

Earlier, he had confided in his father that he wanted to be a band director. His dad had put his arm around his shoulder and said, 'Jim, you know George dropped out of school to go into the army.' Jim nodded. George wanted to get away from home so bad that he lied about his age to get into the military.

'Jim,' his dad continued, 'I'd like to see you go to college.' His dad smiled, but his eyes didn't register any cheer. 'Uh, son.' His dad cleared his throat and began again. 'Well, the truth is we just don't have the money to send you to college.' He gave Jim's shoulder a squeeze and continued with an earnest voice. 'But I really wish you could go.'

When spring rolled around everyone bragged about which university they would attend in the fall. Jim drove himself even harder as he practiced for the annual band concert, his senior year. He locked himself in the bathroom at home and concentrated on Gershwin's *Rhapsody in Blue*. He fluttered his fingers up the knobs of his clarinet perfecting the glissando that introduced the melancholy tune.

He didn't tell his parents about the concert. His dad was traveling on a sales trip and he didn't want his mother to show up drunk. When he got to school he took his place on stage and joined in the cacophony of noise the musicians made as each warmed up to play.

As the lights dimmed Jim felt the surge of nerves butterfly from his chest into his mouth. He grabbed his neck with his left hand to choke down their fluttering, coughed, then cleared his throat several times.

A loud click followed by a low hum accompanied a brilliant spotlight that wavered across the darkness searching for its target. Jim, blinded in its beam, stood for a moment blinking and twitching his fingers on his clarinet. Taking a deep breath, he closed his eyes and imagined the walls of his bathroom surrounding him. He brought the reed to his lips, and began low and soft. Da, da, da, da, daaa! As the music crescendoed up the scale, his heart rose with it and soared into the *Rhapsody in Blue*.

At the close of the concert a man in a well-tailored blue suit elbowed his way to Jim's side. He grabbed him by the right hand and pumped up and down in a firm handshake. 'Son,' he said, flashing white teeth in a wide smile, 'How'd you like to come to the University of Tampa?'

Jim cleared his throat, then glanced over his shoulder. He turned back to the man and tilted the reed of his clarinet at himself. 'Me?' he asked in a high voice. He cleared his throat again and said an octave lower, 'Me?'

The man grinned and continued, 'I'm scouting for talent. Your band director mentioned I might want to come tonight. He said I wouldn't be disappointed and wow!' he slapped Jim on the back. 'I sure wasn't. If you haven't settled on another college, I'm prepared to offer you a full music scholarship to the University of Tampa.'

4

TAR AND FEATHERS

Jim rode the bus on his first day to the university. He leaned forward to get a glimpse of his destination. Moorish minarets set atop the five-story Victorian Palace stood oddly against the Florida skyline. The architectural phenomena dwarfed the surrounding modern buildings which seemed to grovel at its feet.

Jim elbowed the guy next to him. 'Hey, how do you think it was when it was a hotel?' he said with a jerk of his head at the college.

The fellow craned his neck to look up at the onion-shaped domes whose tops sported long spindly fingers that pointed heavenward. 'The Tampa Bay Hotel,' he said in a sing-song tour guide impersonation. 'Once an opulent resort for presidents and queens, now the impressive campus of Tampa University.'

Jim laughed and held out his right hand. 'Jim Kennedy,' he said as introduction.

His companion grasped it in a firm hand shake. 'Billy Campbell. Your first day to the loveliest campus in the South?' Billy flashed a wide smile.

'Yep.' Jim nodded and looked out the window again. He shook his head and whistled. 'What a weird campus. Looks more Russian than Floridian.'

'Hey, Jim,' Billy said punching him on the shoulder. 'I'm going to check out a couple of frats tonight. They're having rush week to choose a new group of pledges. Interested?'

'Sure, it'll be a good way to get to know some guys,' Jim said.

'And girls.' Billy said with a wink. 'I've heard the fraternities and sororities have a lot of parties together.'

'Where do I sign up?' Jim asked with a slow grin.

When Jim found the music school he went directly to meet the band director.

'Good to see you, Jim,' Dr. Wilke said gripping his hand firmly. 'I've been looking forward to having you with us since hearing you play Gershwin.' The director closed his eyes and pantomimed playing the clarinet. 'Doo woo woo woo,' he hummed the opening notes of *Rhapsody in Blue.* 'I've never heard anyone glissade so smoothly.' He thumped Jim on the back and gave him an appreciative grin.

Dr. Wilke motioned toward the chairs in which many students sat playing discordant notes as they warmed up for practice. They approached a short sullen fellow who focused intently on playing his clarinet.

'Jack,' Dr. Wilke said, placing a hand on a young man's shoulder, 'why don't you move over here.' He gestured toward the empty seat beside him. 'I'd like Jim to play first chair clarinet for now.'

Jack looked up as if he'd been stung by a wasp. His mouth dropped open and eyes went wide. 'But, Dr. Wilke, you told me last spring I'd play first chair.'

'Yes, yes, we'll discuss this later.' The professor waved his hand as if shooing a bothersome fly then turned back to Jim. 'Well.' He nodded his head and smiled. 'That's that.' The professor turned and walked briskly back to the director's podium.

Jim held out his right hand. 'Jim Kennedy,' he said with an apologetic grin.

Jack turned his back toward him and began tweedling notes on his clarinet.

'Look,' Jim started, 'I'm sorry about all this. I had no idea –.'

Jack swiveled in his chair and glared at Jim. His thin eyebrows drew together wrinkling his brow into a distorted mask of anger. 'Shut. Up.' He spoke the words separately and deliberately, but Jim heard the pent-up rage underneath their quiet exterior.

Jim picked up his clarinet and began his own warm up. He closed his eyes to block out everything in the room except his music.

Later that afternoon as Jim walked across campus he heard a familiar voice.

'Jim! How's your first day?' Billy jogged over and slapped Jim on the back. 'Hey, I'm heading over to one of those frats. Want to tag along?'

Jim and Billy were welcomed into the fraternity with handshakes and tales of the joys of brotherhood.

'This is the one for me,' Billy said out of the side of his mouth to Jim. 'I heard it's the best on campus.'

Jim shrugged. 'I'm in if you are.'

Billy pulled Jim to a corner of the room and asked, 'But can you take the initiation?' He emphasized each syllable of initiation as if translating Latin.

'I can take whatever they throw at me.' Jim shoved his hands deep in his pockets and bowed out his chest.

A loud cough sounded from the doorway as if someone had choked on a drink. Jim looked up and saw Jack, the second chair clarinetist. 'Oh, no,' he groaned.

As initiation progressed Jim made every effort to avoid contact with Jack. Jack carried a long wooden paddle everywhere he went. He'd swing it back and forth on his index finger as he stalked around campus. Jim ground his teeth whenever the high whining voice called out, 'Assume the position!'

At this command he was required, as a fraternity pledge, to bend over and grab his ankles. Jack seemed to take a perverse pleasure in administering pain. He'd rear back as if at bat in the World Series and swing. The wind whistled impending doom through the drilled holes on the surface of the board before it made contact. Jack laughed each time he hit his rear-end home run. But Jim would straighten quickly and grin down at his shorter foe as if to say, 'That didn't hurt a bit.'

On the final night before initiation the fraternity loaded the pledges into cars and drove miles out of Tampa onto a deserted stretch of road. 'Strip,' they commanded, then handed each fellow a gunny sack to act as loin cloth.

'Raise your arms,' Jack sneered at Jim.

Jim glanced right and left to make sure he wasn't the only one receiving this command. He lifted his hands as if threatened by a dangerous criminal and stared at the top of Jack's head imagining different ways to get him back later. Jack's jealousy had laid deeper roots and blossomed into a poisonous plant when Dr. Wilke handed Jim the coveted baton and declared him drum major of the marching band. Jim led the band expertly and practiced his clarinet and saxophone with diligence knowing his best revenge would be met musically.

Earlier Billy had asked, 'How can you stand being picked on by that runt, Jack? He hates you.'

'Let him do his worst,' Jim responded. 'I'll take him on any day where it really counts.' He twiddled his fingers on an invisible saxophone.

'How do you manage it all?' Billy said with an expansive gesture. 'I barely finish my homework, but you're out all night playing in those dance bands. I bet the girls go wild for you musicians.'

'Girls!' he scoffed. 'I can't watch the dancers when I'm reading music. Plus it's exhausting. When I first started playing with that Latin band I could barely understand what they were saying, much less read the scrap of paper they call music. It was covered in tiny black notes. If you could call them that.'

The notes more closely resembled roudy ants that stomped in ink then danced drunkenly across a tiny scrap of paper. The first time Jim played with them he finished the whole piece five minutes before everyone else. The stage had rocked and rolled under the percussionists' drums. He hadn't experienced an earthquake, but envisioned it feeling similar to the shaking platform they performed on that night. When he went to bed afterward, he dreamed he was sleeping on a raft in the ocean. The sensation of rising and falling wouldn't go away.

Jim rubbed his fingers back and forth against his thumb and grinned. 'But the cash is sweet. And I'm finally out of my folks' place and into a boarding house near campus.'

'You mean the roach motel,' Billy quipped.

'Hey, don't knock it. It's better than living with my mom –' Jim stopped abruptly as if he hadn't meant to open that can of worms. 'And dad,' he added quickly with a forced laugh. 'You know how it is living with your parents.'

Billy gave a hollow laugh. 'I know. I know. I wish I could earn quick cash too. I need money to get out from under my folks.'

The smell of something sickly sweet and rancid filled Jim's nostrils. His mind snapped back to the present where he stood clad only in a gunny sack with his arms raised as if in surrender. The cars had parked in a circle to spotlight the actors in their hideous play. The beams sliced through the darkness which hung heavy and deep in the shadows behind the group of overgrown boys. Jack's eyes shone wolf-like in the eerie glow from the car headlights. He waved a serving spoon dripping with thick sticky goo. His laugh mimicked the timeless playground taunt, 'Neh, neh, neh, neh, neh,' as he glopped the stuff under Jim's arm pits.

Jim gagged and reached to cover his mouth. The muck evidently had been spiked with skunk scent. It not only stunk, it glued his skin and hairs in a wad making it painful to lower his arms.

'Hands in front!' someone shouted.

'You would have made a good drill sergeant,' Jim muttered under his breath.

'That's, 'Yes, Drill Sergeant, Sir,' to you, Jimbo,' Jack said with a smirk.

Jim presented his hands for handcuffs. He was rewarded with more of the rancid goo which gummed around his fingers. He smiled in spite of himself remembering the story of Brer Rabbit and the Tar Baby. The fraternity brothers then coated the pledges' bare feet with the tar before dumping pillow cases of feathers over their heads. They whooped and danced around batting at feathers and laughing at the spectacle they had created.

The feathers swirled white and thick in the beams of the headlights before being drawn inexorably to the sticky tar. The fraternity brothers laughed and jeered at the unfortunate pledges. As they cavorted, Jim kept his eyes straight ahead and wondered how he'd allowed himself to be caught up in this odd rite of passage. He made an effort to detach himself and watch the surroundings as a spectator. To his left Billy held his elbows out at an awkward angle. 'You look like a half-plucked chicken,' Jim said, and grinned despite his own discomfort.

'Let's go, boys!' The frat boys yelled and ran to their cars, started their engines and roared away in a cloud of dust. The tarred and feathered pledges stared silently at the retreating tail lights. The chirping of crickets and blurping of frogs, which had been drowned out by shouting, suddenly grew loud in the quiet. The pledges turned and stared at each other.

'You should see how ridiculous you look.' Billy pointed at Jim with a forced laugh.

'Buddy, you need a mirror,' Jim countered.

'Sh,' someone hissed, 'listen.'

The distant hum of tires on asphalt droned from the opposite direction their 'brothers' had taken.

'Somebody's coming,' one fellow whispered.

'Hey, if we flag them down we won't have to walk all the way back to Tampa,' Billy yelled and began to hop up and down waving his arms.

The other boys collectively held their breath as the car approached. When the headlights fell on their group they were unable to constrain themselves. They waved their arms and called, 'Hey! Help! We need a ride.'

The car slowed. But as the boys rushed forward, they saw a face staring wild-eyed from the interior.

'Go, go, go!' a terrified voice in the car shouted, and the engine roared as the driver gunned the accelerator.

'Wait! Stop!' the group yelled as they jumped out of the way.

'Remind me why I joined *this* fraternity,' Jim said as he watched the red tail lights fade in the distance.

'Aw, quit complainin',' Billy said with a grunt as he stepped on a rock. 'We've got a long way to go.'

'Wonder how far away from town we are?'

'I heard one of the brothers say it was about fifteen miles,' someone volunteered.

'Fifteen miles,' everyone groaned.

Jim felt the skin had worn off his feet as the first rays crept up the horizon. 'Look,' someone called, 'the minarets!' The pointed domes of the university stood in silhouette against the rosy hue of the sunrise.

'I've got it all figured out,' Billy said. 'If you'll throw in some cash, I know where we can get a boat pretty cheap. We could start our own water-ski school and tourists will pay through the nose for a half hour on the boards.'

Jim's shoulders sagged. 'I'm too exhausted to argue, Billy. Whatever you say. I'll have to spend a week in the water anyway to get this skunk scent off. I'm sure my band-mates will be delighted when I show up smelling so pleasant,' he said sarcastically.

The next night the pledges paraded into the fraternity as full members. The brothers had promised a wild party to celebrate. When the lights went out, Jim wasn't sure what to expect, but what he saw made him sick.

He turned to Billy and grimaced. 'I can't believe I went through all that pain and suffering for this.' He gestured to the front of the room where a white screen reflected the images from a movie camera.

'This is disgusting. I'm out of here.' Jim stood to go, but Jack snatched his shirttail.

'What's wrong,' he slurred, 'You won't watch naked women? You some kind of pansy?' His breath reeked of alcohol.

Jim shoved him hard and Jack stumbled backward knocking over the projector. Shouts and curses chorused from the group. Jim wanted to spit on the floor to rid his mouth of the bad taste left by this ridiculous fraternity.

He turned on his heel and never looked back.

5

HELP WANTED

'Hit it!' the skier yelled from the water.

Jim slammed the throttle forward. The front end of the boat kicked upward as the motor roared in its effort to yank its burden out of the water.

'Wow! This sure is powerful,' said a pretty young woman who perched in the seat next to Jim. 'Hold on, sweetie,' she shouted over the noise of the engine and wind as she clung to her towheaded five-year-old boy.

'You've got a lot of customers,' she said. 'We're grateful for the boat ride. Sammy would have cried all day if he hadn't gotten to sit in the passenger seat. Wouldn't you, baby?' She tickled the child who giggled and slid down in his seat.

Jim nodded and glanced over his shoulder to check the progress of the skier. The skinny boy hunched forward with a strained expression on his face as he clutched the handle of the tow rope. He let go with his right hand, raised it in a quick wave at the crowd on shore, then grabbed hold once more.

'How long have you been operating this water-ski school?' she asked as she ran her long fingers through her son's tousled hair.

Jim fixed his eyes in front to negotiate a turn. 'My buddy and I just started this operation a few weeks ago. We went in together to buy the boat. We're both students at Tampa University and thought this would be a great part-time job.'

The woman tittered a high-pitched laugh and pointed. 'That ski belt is a little big for him, don't you think?'

Jim looked back again and saw the skier bowing his legs to keep the belt from dropping to his ankles.

'I'd better swing him back,' Jim said. He motioned to the boy that they would head back to shore. The skier nodded vigorously as he made an effort to pull the belt up to his waist.

After releasing the skier to coast to the beach, Jim twisted the steering wheel in a hard turn to bring the boat back to the pier. A cry of alarm startled him. He hadn't noticed the woman had left her seat to climb onto the forward deck of the boat. When he veered, she had lost her balance and now slid toward the water.

Her face, frozen in a mask of terror, made Jim lose his head. He would later relive that memory again and again kicking himself for his stupidity. He let go of the wheel and lunged toward the woman in a desperate grab. The moment he released the steering, the boat bucked and twisted violently, then a wall of water washed over him.

At first Jim thought they had taken on a heavy wave. But when he realized what happened he slapped the water in anger. He had been thrown from the boat.

Jim spun around to get his bearings and gasped. The boat, bow tilting up at a thirty-degree angle, roared at top speed toward the crowd on the beach. He heard their shrieks and shouts over the lapping of the water and the noise of the engine. The small boy sat alone in the stern. He reached toward Jim with chubby arms and wailed, 'Mommy! Mommy!'

The trailing tow line popped and skipped over the top of the water to his right and Jim dove for it. He swam, pulling hard and fast to reach it before it was too late. 'Almost, almost,' Jim said with each stroke. The rope was inches from his fingertips.

'Help! I can't swim!' a frantic feminine voice shouted behind him.

'Oh, Lord!' Jim groaned. 'What's next?'

Without hesitation he spun around and swam toward the thrashing woman. When he was still fifteen feet away, her head sank beneath the waves, drowning her cries. He put his own head down and windmilled his arms quickly and smoothly through the water. 'Go, go, go!' His shouts bubbled from his mouth in a cloud of foam. His lungs burned with the effort of reaching the woman before she drowned.

'Where is she?' he shouted as he spun around looking in every direction. He had arrived at the point where he'd seen her last, but the woman had disappeared.

'Whoa!' he spluttered when he suddenly was grabbed from behind and jerked under.

'Help me!' The woman cried out hoarsely between gasping for air and coughing violently.

'Take it easy!' Jim tried to calm her, but his voice was edged with frustration. 'Let me go. You're pulling me under.'

He pried her rigid fingers off his neck, seeing with a grimace that her fist clutched a wad of his hair. His scalp stung where she'd yanked it out. He flipped her over and towed her toward the shore. 'It will be easier on both of us if you just relax,' he said through gritted teeth.

'My baby! My baby!' She tried to twist around to see what had become of the boat.

The steering wheel must have held a slight turn after Jim had been ejected. Instead of heading for the crowded beach it had veered left. Jim watched in horror as it ran aground on a high bank covered with dense undergrowth. The flat bottom skimmed up the embankment and the craft disappeared on the other side.

Jim felt the sandy bottom under his toes and shoved the distraught mother toward the shore. He ran through the shallows with her following behind calling frantically, 'Sammy! Sammy!'

A thin gray wisp of smoke snaked up through the undergrowth, signaling the accident. The motor whined loud and high like a wounded animal. In his mind's eye Jim imagined pulling the boy's mangled body out of the wreckage and placing it in the weeping mother's arms.

'Oh, please no,' he whispered under his breath and shook his head to dispel the image.

The crowd on the shore, which had been frozen in shock as they watched the spectacle unfold, now ran toward the smoke. Shouts of, 'Hurry! Save the child!' rang over the engine noise.

Jim dashed down the shore then jerked to a stop as if he had slammed into an invisible barrier. There before him was the last thing he could have imagined. It flashed past and leapt at the woman behind him.

'Mommy! Mommy!' the little boy shouted. 'Can we do that again!'

Jim hunched forward, grabbing his knees and breathing heavily. His hair rained drops of brackish water into the sand, and his shoulders sagged in relief. Then, jerking his head up, he sucked air in deeply. 'The boat!' he growled and took off running again.

He climbed the embankment toward the whine of the engine. There it was. It lay cradled on top of a bent tree. Jim jumped into the driver's seat and shut off the engine. Several spectators rushed around him.

The skinny skier was one of the first on the scene. 'Would you look at that!' he said with a laugh. 'Hardly a scratch on it.'

Early the next morning Jim rose with the sun. He threw on a jacket and jogged down to the water for crew practice. Other early risers congregated like dark shadows around the small boat house. 'Hi, Jim,' one greeted.

'Hey, Albert,' Jim said, and covered his mouth to stifle a yawn.

'Late night, huh,' Albert asked.

'Rough week,' Jim answered. He stared at the mist hovering over the surface of the water and shivered. It reminded him too much of the smoke billowing from the wrecked ski boat the day before.

Albert laughed. 'Yeah, I heard about the excitement at the lake yesterday.'

Jim raised his eyebrows. 'Excitement, ha. Is that what you'd call it? I'd call it heart failure.'

They bent down with several others and lifted a long thin scull and carried it to the water, which was black as oil in the dim morning light. Jim threw off his jacket. 'Brr,' he said as he rubbed his arms. 'Why do we have to practice so early?'

Albert beat his chest in a Tarzan imitation. 'Makes you strong.'

Jim reached up and grabbed his left elbow and twisted to the right. He repeated the stretch with his left arm then bent to touch his toes. The rest of the crew team warmed up in a similar fashion stretching their arms and backs to limber up.

The eight rowers stepped gingerly into the scull and pulled their large oars into place. The coxswain began barking orders and all swept forward and back in an even rhythm. The swish and drip of the water was oddly comforting. Each member of the team pulled together, operating as a single unit simulating a large water bug gliding gracefully over the surface of the lake.

Jim slid forward in a crouch before shoving back, straightening his knees, and pulling on the long oar with all his might. His breath came in a cadence that matched the coxswain's call. The knot that had wound around his rib cage after the boat accident the day before unwound as they slipped swiftly through the water. He pushed himself hard, revelling in the pain of the workout. The coxswain applauded the crew's efforts. 'You guys are gonna win this weekend. We're flying!'

Jim packed as much as he could into his first two years at the university. He ran himself ragged between school work, leading the marching band as drum major, playing in the Latin band, running a ski school, rowing on the crew team, weight lifting and boxing. Whatever he did, Jim strove for excellence.

During the summer after his sophomore year he worked on a construction job. Those guys swinging hammers as they framed houses sported dark tans and acted carefree as they whistled at girls on the sidewalks. Jim thought it would be brainless work where he could quickly rack up a lot of money.

He had succeeded in everything he put his hand to, but the construction workers were not impressed with his building skills. They relegated him to cart the scaffolding from trucks to job sites where he assembled towers on which the skilled laborers stood. Each metal bar weighed close to one hundred pounds. Jim's old football injury complained under the load as he ferried section after section and bolted them together.

When he was not hauling scaffolding, he caulked baseboards. Inside the new buildings the heat topped one hundred degrees. He wiped the excess caulk off the walls with a rag, but invariably it would gum up his fingers. It was not long before he zebra-striped his pants in an effort to rid his hands of the sticky goo.

After a few weeks of hard labor he grabbed a newspaper to check the help-wanted ads. On a short break, Jim dropped on the sidewalk and took a long swig of a warm Coke. The bubbles fizzed and burned his throat as he tried to quench his thirst. He wiped his sweating brow with the tail of his T-shirt, then rustled through the newspaper to look for a different job.

On the first page of the ads in large bold print were the words: 'Arthur Murray Dance Studios are currently seeking individuals who desire a career as a dance instructor. We are hiring both part-time and full-time teachers. Past experience not necessary. We will train you. Opportunities for advancement in our organization also available.'

Jim checked his watch and groaned. 'Aw, man. I've got six more hours till quitting time.'

'Hey, buddy.' A lean construction worker called. 'How 'bout finishin' this scaffolding. We're waitin' on ya.' By his accent Jim imagined the man had just migrated south from the Bronx. His pasty white skin confirmed he was no Florida native.

Jim smiled. He knew the obnoxious fellow would be sun burned lobster red by the end of the day.

'Retribution,' Jim said under his breath.

'Whatcha sayin', buddy?' The worker shoved his hands in his pockets and leaned against the building. An inch of ash jiggled on the end of the cigarette he balanced on his lower lip.

'Nothin',' Jim said with a grunt as he shoved an iron bar onto the scaffold tower.

That evening Jim showered quickly before taking the bus to the Arthur Murray dance studio. He paused at the bottom of the steps to read the bill posted on the wall.

Seeking individuals who :
- *Are outgoing and energetic*
- *Have a good personality*
- *Have good communication skills*
- *Have a positive attitude*
- *Enjoy working with people and helping them*
- *Are motivated and goal-oriented*
- *Are team players*
- *And like to have fun.*

An hour later Jim skipped back down the stairs clutching several sheets of paper in his right hand. He beamed down at the top page. It read, 'New dance instructor's training schedule.' He kicked out sideways clicking his heels together and whooped. 'Goodbye, construction job, hello...' he broke off as he held his arms aloft in a dancing pose. He Fred-Astaired the box step in a quick one, two, three. 'Hello, dream job.'

6

DANCE WITH ME

With Jim's musical background and his sense of rhythm and timing he had a leg up on the other potential Arthur Murray instructors. He soon danced his way to the head of the class. It was not long before he was twirling pretty girls across the floor of the second-story studio in downtown Tampa.

His pockets bulged with cash on payday, and he spent every available hour signing up new clients. When fall rolled around Jim dusted off his clarinet and saxophone and headed back to the university.

After a few weeks Dr. Wilke, pulled him aside. 'Jim, what's wrong. I can tell your body is here, but your head is somewhere else. If you want to keep first chair I'd better see you trying a little harder.' He stood back and eyed Jim up and down. 'Look at you, boy,' he said shaking his head. 'Did you sleep in your clothes? They're one mass of wrinkles. Your eyes have dark circles under them, and....' He paused a moment, then as if he remembered something, crossed his arms and added, 'And what was with the ...' he side-pranced back and forth, 'the fancy footwork on the field Saturday night. You're a drum major, not Fred Astaire.'

'You know, Dr. Wilke,' Jim said. 'I always wanted to be just like you or Mr. Lucas, my high school band teacher. I love to play and wanted to be a director. But after trying to lead the college choir in that choral piece last week I realized this just isn't the job for me.'

Dr. Wilke raised his conductor's baton as if Jim had challenged him to a duel. He raised his chin and looked down his nose. 'What are you talking about? You are an incredibly talented musician. I have never heard any one with better technique.'

Jim tilted his head sideways and gave a half smile. 'Technique, yes,' he said with a sigh. He tapped the side of his head. 'But, no ear –.' His voice trailed off and he stared over his professor's shoulder at the wall.

'But you are a marvelous musician, Jim. There are many other –'

'No, sir,' Jim interrupted. He sliced his hand through the air cutting off the protest. 'I've made up my mind. I've found something else I love more than music. Plus the pay is great.' His chin came up and he looked his band director directly in the eye. 'I'm working at the Arthur Murray dance studio. They say I've got a good chance of becoming a manager in a year or so if I keep it up.'

Dr. Wilke stepped back. 'Dance instructor? Jim, you can't throw away a college education to twirl silly young women around.'

'I'm still in school. I'm not quitting the university,' Jim assured him.

But a few months later Jim decided the only schooling he needed was what Arthur Murray offered at the studio. After calculating how much time it would take to advance from instructor to supervisor to marketing and managing his own studio, he promptly quit the University of Tampa.

Dance fever had swept through America like the plague. In the late 40's it infected over three million of the younger generation transforming wallflowers into ballroom socialites. Murray too had dropped his intended profession as an architect in favor of dancing. Everyone knew about Arthur Murray. He was listed in *Who's Who in America* every year. With his how-to-do-it books topping the best-seller list twice and studios scattered across America, Murray had amassed a fortune.

Jim made money hand-over-fist, but it burned holes in his pockets. He spent it as fast as he made it. First he moved out of the old boarding house near campus and into an apartment closer to the studio. Next he waved at passengers on the city bus from behind the wheel of the car he purchased.

'See those poor guys on that bus? That was me only a few months ago,' he said glancing sideways at the pretty girl riding next to him in the passenger seat.

'I think I'll come take some lessons at the studio,' she said.

'Well, if you do, that means we can't go out any more,' Jim said with a shrug.

'Why not?' his date asked in a high-pitched squeal.

'Instructors can't date students.' He stretched out his right arm across the back of her seat and said in a fatherly tone, 'Bad for business. If the couple broke up, Arthur Murray would lose a good customer.' His white teeth flashed a wide grin.

'Oh, Jim! Does that mean we are dating?' she asked snuggling into the crook of his arm.

Jim sat up and jerked his arm back to grip the steering wheel at ten and two with both hands. He glanced sideways at the smiling girl.

'Let's not get too hasty,' he said with a laugh. 'This is just our second date. I am too busy for a steady girlfriend. Maybe you should come take those lessons after all.'

The girl crossed her arms and sat rigid in the seat. 'Maybe I don't want to go dancing tonight after all,' she said sarcastically and poked out her lower lip.

'Aw, honey. You'll love this spot. It's right on the beach. I went there last summer and saw everyone doing this dance.' He let go of the wheel with his right hand and gestured a semicircle. He leaned forward and his eyes gleamed with a sparkle. 'I couldn't figure out what they were doing with their feet. It seemed so complicated.' He sat back and laughed. 'That was one of the first dances they taught us as instructors. It's pie.' He gestured with a flick of his hand.

'Pie?' his date asked arching her brows.

'In, as easy as,' he explained.

'Oh! Jim,' she said with a giggle. 'You're so cute when you talk that way. Pie!' she squeaked. 'Easy as pie. I'll have to remember that one.'

Jim glanced to the left out his driver's side window and rolled his eyes.

Later that month his brother George came home on leave from the army. 'Let's go find a party,' he said and grabbed the car keys from Jim's hand.

'You're not doing too badly, little brother,' he said. 'This is a pretty sweet car. How much did it cost you?'

'It's-,' Jim began.

'Hey, look at them fruitcakes,' his brother interrupted. 'Hey, you Navy pansies!' George shouted out the window. 'Nice girlie white sailor suits!' He turned to Jim and laughed. 'Ha! Those Navy boys think they're such hot stuff. We army men have to show them who's boss.'

George wheeled into a parking spot in front of a nightclub. 'Hey, this should be a hot spot! Let's check it out Jimmy boy.'

Jim looked up at the garish neon sign that blared from the club's front window. He felt like a little kid around his older brother. When he got out of the car and turned to shut the door he heard quick footsteps behind him and saw a flash of white.

Later, when he reflected on what followed, everything seemed to happen in slow motion although he knew it took only seconds. A face distorted with anger had loomed above him like an angry deity. A ham-sized fist swung 'a four.' The boxing lingo flashed through his mind at the time: one being the left hand jab, two – right punch, three – left hook, and four was the upper cut the sailor used to unhinge his jaw.

He did not remember anything after that except a brilliant flash of light when a bomb exploded behind his retinas. He did remember George peeling him off the sidewalk and folding him back into the passenger seat.

'Quit your moaning,' he chided.

'My jaw,' Jim groaned feeling the bone that jacked sideways up to the middle of his ear. 'I need to go to the hospital,' he mumbled in pain.

'Turn this way. Let me see it,' George said.

Jim twisted his body to face his brother.

'Pishh! That's nothin'." George grabbed Jim's jaw with his meaty hand and yanked it sideways with a violent jerk.

'Ow!' Jim yelled. 'What did you...?'

'All fixed,' George interrupted.

Jim scowled at his brother with narrowed eyes. He cradled his jaw in his right and said, 'You just....'

'Look,' George said and turned the rear view mirror toward Jim.

Jim leaned forward and gazed bleary-eyed into the rectangular mirror. He opened and closed his mouth several times with both hands pressed on either side of his face. 'Hmm, it pops.'

'Yeah, but it works fine. Just call me Doc. I won't answer to George the rest of the night. Let's try this place,' George said, stopping abruptly in front of another garish night club.

'Just don't insult any more people while I'm around you. Please,' Jim added. He glanced up and down the street before getting out the passenger door.

Throughout the next year Jim moved up the Arthur Murray corporate ladder rapidly. He began making a name for himself as a real go-getter. He had worked his way into a management position when one day his destiny walked through the door. It came in a smaller package than he had imagined, but there was no doubt his life would change. At five feet two with flashing eyes of blue and wavy chocolate-brown locks, a girl walked in and captured his heart.

Anne Lewis had come with a date to Jim's studio. Her boyfriend had been taking lessons to impress her. On Friday nights students invited their dates to the open-dance party at the studio. He brought Anne to watch him strut his stuff. She sat in a chair in the main ballroom to wait for him to finish his private instruction in another room.

In the main ballroom Jim drove a matronly woman around the dance floor when his eyes caught Anne's. She immediately looked away, but he didn't. He auto-piloted his partner expertly for the best view of the new girl who sat demurely in a chair against the wall.

At the end of the song, he bowed and thanked the woman for giving him that wonderful dance. Bee-lining toward the refreshment table, Jim met a fellow instructor.

'See that girl over there?' he asked, staring at her over his punch glass. He hummed the tune to Frank Sinatra's hit song then sang softly, 'Will I ever find the girl on my mind, the one who is my ideal? Maybe she's a dream, and yet she might be just around the corner waiting for me. Da, da, do, How's the rest of it go? Oh, never mind. There she is. Look.' He pointed toward Anne with his chin. 'She's my ideal. I'm going to marry her.' He slammed his cup down to emphasize his words. The juice sloshed out wetting the white table cloth.

'Watch it, Kennedy,' his friend warned. He dabbed the spill with a napkin. 'You know the policy. You're the manager for Pete's sake. No dating clients.'

'Well how else will I get to know her unless I convince her to buy some time with me on the dance floor.'

'You could sell the complete set of *Encyclopedia Britannica* to an illiterate blind man, Jim. I'm sure you won't have any trouble convincing that little lady. Just don't date her till her lessons are finished.'

Jim scoffed. 'You don't have to tell me. I'm the manager, remember?'

Anne's escort came out, flushed with the heat of dancing. He shoved back the hair that clung to his sweating brow in wet curls and said between breaths, 'Hey, hon. Why don't you take a dance proficiency analysis. I bet you could dance circles around most people here.

Anne smiled and pushed a waving lock of hair behind an ear. 'Well, I would have wasted my parents' money if I hadn't learned something all those years I studied dance.'

'I thought you were just practicing for the ski ballet you performed at Lake Hollingsworth,' he said chucking her under the chin.

'Hey, ask the teacher to give you an evaluation. He's the head dance guru at this joint,' he said, jerking his thumb in Jim's direction.

'Oh he is,' Anne turned in Jim's direction and smiled.

A moment later, Jim led her onto the floor, placed a hand on her slim waist and cradled her right in his left. 'You follow well,' he complimented. 'Have you had much formal instruction?'

'Not this kind of instruction,' she said, looking up at him through her long lashes.

He swallowed hard in an effort to keep himself from howling. 'You're very good,' he said in a soft purr. 'I think with just a few lessons you could be great.'

'Really?' she asked as she opened her eyes wide. The light danced in their blue irises and Jim saw his reflection in their depths. At her command he would have jumped through hoops.

He swung her around in a quick spin, and her red lips parted in a giddy laugh. He turned his head and looked in the other direction in order to restrain himself from pressing his own lips against hers.

A running dialogue of saint and devil argued in his mind. 'Jim,' said the saint. 'Get hold of yourself. You've never reacted to a girl like this. You don't even know her.'

The devil yelled louder, 'Kiss her you fool.' Jim grinned at the devil's words.

Her eyes widened and she pushed away from him. 'Are you laughing at me?'

Jim scoffed. 'Laughing, hardly. I'm just delighted to have the opportunity to dance with you. You are the most promising first-time dancer I've ever encountered. Listen, I'll give you our bargain special. Just don't mention it to anyone else. For only one hundred dollars I'll give you ten hours of instruction.'

'One hundred dollars is a bargain?' Her voice ran up the scale at the question.

'Guarantee it,' Jim said with his winningest smile.

She cleared her throat. 'Do I have to pay tonight?'

'No, bring it to our first lesson. How about Monday? I think I could squeeze you into my busy schedule.'

7

REBUKED

Jim waited for Anne's lesson each week as if she were Santa coming with a bag of treats. The days dragged their feet and the hours lasted days before her arrival. But the time of her lesson flew by in seconds. Then came the long wait for her next visit.

Jim taught her expertly and listened better than any bartender to her life story.

'What haven't you done?' he asked one day. 'So far I gather you grew up in a zoo.'

She slapped his shoulder, 'Jim! Really,' she scoffed. 'I said my dad is a vet not a zoo keeper.'

'You told me he collected animals of all sizes and descriptions,' he said feigning surprise.

'To work on,' she said, emphasizing *work*. 'That's what vets do, you know. His practice was at our house in Lakeland. He also built boats. That's how I got into water-skiing.'

'Remind me to tell you about the ski school a buddy and I ran here in Tampa,' Jim said. 'No, step forward, back, forward two, three, four. Yes! That's it. You're a quick learner.'

'Ski school, tell me now,' Anne begged.

'Not now, you talk and I'll teach. Take my right hand and spin. Yes, good! You're a cow-girl too. Is that right, or did you hunt foxes in a red coat and top hat?'

'No, silly. Just because I rode horses doesn't make me a cow-girl, and I didn't hunt foxes. I've never seen one in Lakeland. Maybe there are foxes in the vineyards though.'

'Vineyards?'

'Yes, you know. It says it in the Bible, 'The little foxes spoil the grapes.''

'So you're a preacher too?' Jim asked as he dipped her backward.

'I could never stand up in front of a bunch of people and speak. But I do sing in the church choir. I was a music major at Birmingham Southern College in Alabama.'

Jim stopped abruptly. 'Me too! But not in Birmingham, of course.'

'You sang in the church choir?' Anne asked with wide eyes.

'No, hardly.' He gripped her again and danced across the floor. 'I was a music major.' He twirled her and started in another direction. 'At Tampa University,' he continued. 'I played clarinet and sax.'

'Me too!' Anne squeaked.

'Oh dear, did I step on your toes? What caused you to squeal?' He stuck his index finger in his ear and wiggled it in a circle.

'I did not squeal. I just can't believe we both played the clarinet.'

'Yes. It won me fame and fortune. That is, a scholarship and a spot in a famous local Latin band. But, I gave it all up at the call of Terpsichore.'

'Twerpy what?'

'The Greek Muse of dancing and choral song,' Jim said with a scoff. 'You ought to know your Greek muses, especially this one. I doubt you were really a music major.'

'You tease,' she said and stomped his toe.

He grabbed it and hopped around the room on the other foot.

'I not only graduated in music, but I also taught at my alma mata for a few years after traveling with my girlfriends on a European tour.'

'You're just rubbing it in. I didn't graduate. I followed my mentor Arthur Murray. He gave up his profession too.'

'Mentor? No way! You've met him?' Anne stared open-mouthed and shoved Jim with both hands. He stumbled backward pretending she was the sailor who belted him with a right uppercut.

She ran forward, grabbed his arm and pulled him back to the center of the floor. 'Stop it. I didn't push you that hard.'

Jim raised a restraining hand. 'Now, Anne, don't get so excited. I haven't met him yet, but I will when I win the Arthur Murray All-American dance competition.'

'Really?' Anne looked at him admiringly. 'When is that going to be?'

'You realize this is your last lesson.' Jim evaded her question. 'If you buy the Bronze Medal course you might be able to come to the competition here in Tampa.'

'How much is this Bronze Medal Course?' Anne asked.

'It's really a bargain. You can't pass it up. You are getting so good, it would be a shame not to keep going.'

'Okay, okay. You don't have to lay it on so thick. Just tell me how much.'

'It's worth more than it costs. You could really go far with the Bronze Medal. Let me show you what all you will learn.'

Anne went into Jim's office and studied the papers that outlined the dances she would learn when she took the Bronze Medal Course. At the bottom of the page in small print was the price – five hundred dollars.

She gulped several times before saying in a small voice, 'I think I could come up with the money.'

Anne didn't tell Jim until much later that she asked her old boyfriend from Birmingham to float her a loan for the lessons. Jim wasn't sure Anne was as mad about him as he was with her and wanted to keep her coming back as often as possible. The Bronze Medal Course insured him at least six more months.

It wasn't long after beginning her bronze medal course that she addressed a scented blue note card to Mr. James Kennedy, Arthur Murray's Studio of Dancing, Lafayette Street, Tampa, Florida.

Dear Mr. Kennedy,
I just wanted to write you a note and wish for you the happiest new year ever.

I'm enjoying my lessons so much and consider myself extremely fortunate for having such an outstanding instructor.

Best wishes.
Sincerely,
Anne Lewis

This began three-and-a-half years of correspondence between Jim and Anne.

The frequency of the letters between the two and the warmth of the messages increased steadily.

Jim couldn't sell Anne the silver or gold medal classes, because he had broken the cardinal rule – teachers don't date students. But they still danced together as often as Anne could take the train from her home in Lakeland to Tampa to meet him.

'I've ridden on that 5:30 train for five consecutive Saturdays. The conductor must think I live in Tampa and just go home on the weekends,' she complained to Jim. 'Why don't you drive over to Lakeland tomorrow and come to church with my family?'

Jim laughed. 'Church! I haven't been to church since I was a little kid in Chicago. Once I was the only one to show up for the Sunday School class. The teacher loaded me in his car and we drove to a field and sat under a tree for the hour. That was the best Sunday School class I have ever been to.' He threw back his shoulders and said in an authoritative voice, 'You don't have to go to a church to be a good person.' He cleared his throat and spoke as from a recitation. 'You can be just as good a Christian without going to church.'

Anne pushed him. 'Oh, no you can't, Jim Kennedy,' she said with her brows knit together and her mouth set in a tight frown of disapproval.

Jim gaped as if his pet lamb had just bitten him on the ankle. 'I've never known anybody who considered church to be important one way or another,' he said, his voice registering incredulity that she had the audacity to disagree with him.

'Come to think of it,' he said studying the ceiling, 'I don't think I know anyone who goes to church at all, besides you, of course. Oh, yeah,' he stopped for a moment and closed his eyes as if trying to remember. 'There was Mr. Lucas, my high school band director. He was always asking us to go to church with him.'

That Saturday night Jim stumbled into his apartment. His head pounded from the constant blaring of dance rhythms. He pulled off his shirt and dropped it on the living-room floor, and shuffled down the hall kicking off his shoes as he went. Loosening his belt, he dropped his pants and left them puddled on his bedroom floor. After he collapsed into bed, he reached up and fumbled with the lamp to turn it out.

'I can't keep this up,' he mumbled into his pillow. 'These all-night dance parties are going to be the death of me.' Jerking up suddenly, he glared at the clock-radio beside his bed. He flopped his hand onto it and twiddled the dial to a soothing station. The last thing Jim remembered was setting the alarm for a much later wake-up time than usual.

8

RADIO RELIGION

'Behold I stand at the door and knock.' A voice thundered.

Jim bolted up from his rumpled pillow. 'Wh -?' he mumbled. 'Who's there?'

'If anyone hears my voice and opens the door, I'll come in.' The booming voice continued.

Jim shook his head and rubbed his eyes. 'What time is it?'

'Now!' the voice continued, 'is the time for salvation.'

'Ugh!' Jim groaned. 'What station is this? Where's Guy Lombardo with the sweetest music *this* side of heaven. I didn't want to wake up to some raving preacher exercising his larynx.'

He lunged to twist the knob on the radio. However, his hand froze midair before it touched the dial. The radio preacher bellowed in a loud voice, 'Young man, if you were to die tonight and stand before Almighty God and He asked you, "What right do you have to come into My Heaven?" What would you say?'

Jim sat back and stared at the radio and thought, *I've lived a good life. I'm better than most folks I know. I've tried to follow the golden rule.*

The preacher took a breath and continued, 'The young lieutenant to whom I asked this question responded, "I've lived a good life and followed the golden rule."'

Jim nodded and laid back on the bed and grinned. 'I haven't gone to church in years and even I knew the right answer to that question.'

But the preacher's voice interrupted his self-congratulations. 'Young man, if you had the audacity to say such a thing to an all holy God, who knows your every thought and deed, He would have instantly plunged you into the everlasting Lake of Fire.' His voice trembled with zeal.

Jim sat up and stared at the radio in disbelief as the preacher told his radio audience the only way to receive eternal life was to accept it as a gift from God. 'You can never be good enough to please God. So God sent his own Son, Jesus Christ to pay the penalty for your sin. Jesus suffered and died in our place. If you will accept His payment for your sin by inviting Him into your life as Savior and Lord, God will let you into heaven.'

Jim laughed. *That guy's crazy. They should kick him off the radio. Everybody knows you can't get something for free, especially not salvation from God.*

He massaged his brow with his fingers and remembered Anne's rebuke. 'You can't be a good Christian without going to church!'

What if I died? he said to himself, *And God asked me what right do I have to get into heaven? Why shouldn't I go to heaven?* he thought, *I'm no criminal. I haven't done anything really bad.*

As if reading his thoughts the radio pastor spoke in an authoritative voice, 'No one is perfect except God. We all have sinned and fall short of the glory and perfection of God.'

'What if a man decided to enter your home at three o'clock in the morning by putting up a ladder to your second-floor window. You would be inclined to shoot such an intruder, who obviously could claim no right to come into your house. What do you think God is going to do,' the preacher asked, 'when you attempt to climb through some back window, when He has already told you that Christ Jesus is the door and there is no other access? Jesus said, "Those who come to the Father must come by me." There is no other way into heaven.'

Jim whiffed out a breath as though someone punched him in the gut. He ran his fingers back and forth through his hair till it stood up at odd angles. The curtain that veiled eternity had been jerked back and he shuddered at what he saw on the other side.

'Dr. Donald Gray Barnhouse of the Tenth Presbyterian Church in Philadelphia will return in a moment after station identification,' the radio announced.

Jim hoped to hear more, but after the commercial break the program was finished. He flipped the switch off and began to pace his small room. 'I've got everything I want. I'm raking in $750 a week. Why is what that preacher said eating me?' he asked himself.

The next day before heading up the stairs to the studio he stopped at a curbside newsstand. 'You got any books about religion?' he asked the scruffy-faced man who sat on a stool behind the counter.

The man scratched the stubble on his cheeks and said, 'Hm, religion. That's an unusual request.' He turned and ran his finger up and down the wall of books and magazines. 'Here's something,' he said lifting up a thick hardback book. 'The Greatest Story Ever Told,' he said, peering at the title through his bifocals. 'I think this is a religious book. You want it?'

Jim laid down the money and grabbed up the book. He watched the clock all day. Never before had he been anxious for a day at the studio to end, but he could not wait to get into the book. That night he devoured several chapters before he fell asleep with the lamp glowing in the darkness and the book cradled in his hand on his pillow. Each night he repeated the procedure until the weekend rolled around.

Saturday afternoon several of his studio buddies knocked on his office door. 'Hey Jim, we're all heading to the Coconut Club tonight. There's supposed to be a ripping band. You've got the biggest car. Why don't you drive us there?'

Jim shook his head. 'Not tonight. I've got to catch up on some reading.'

One of them walked into the room and laid a hand on his forehead. 'He's burning up. I think he's delirious.'

'Cut it out,' Jim said with a laugh and batted his buddy's hand away. He leaned back in his chair, clasped his fingers behind his head and smirked at his surprised friends. 'Hey, it's not like I go out every Saturday night.'

'Yes, you do,' a dark-haired instructor said as she nodded her head. 'I've been here two years and I've never known you to stay home on a Saturday night.'

'Well, its high time I did then,' he said and pushed himself out of his chair. 'Close your mouths. You're going to catch flies. I haven't lost my mind. I'm just staying home. Is that a crime?'

'No, no,' they chorused and moved away quickly, looking back over their shoulders as if he'd sprouted wings or grown a horn in the center of his head.

Jim shook his head and laughed to himself. 'I guess I have been quite the party guy.'

That night he read how Jesus willingly died a horrendous, gruesome death to pay the penalty for his sins so that he, Jim Kennedy, could know God and go to heaven when he died.

He slipped out of his chair, fell on his knees and clasped his hands as a beggar pleading for his life. 'I'm sorry,' he said in a choked voice. 'Oh, God, I'm *so* sorry. I didn't know. I didn't know what you had done for me. Forgive me. Forgive me,' He bent forward till his head touched the floor. 'Come into my heart and never let me forget what you have done for me.'

When he awoke the next morning, he thought, 'I should go to church. But where should I go?'

He grabbed the phone book and looked under churches. 'Wow,' he said with a whistle. 'Look at all these churches listed. I didn't realize there were so many Christians in Tampa. I wonder why I haven't come across any.'

His eyes lighted on a name of one church and he paused. He tapped his finger on the page, 'That looks familiar. I think I remember that was where my high school band director was choir director.'

He dressed quickly and wrote down the address of the church before jumping in his car to make the 11:00 service. He found a seat near the front and waited for the preacher to open the Bible and reveal its secrets.

Thirty minutes later when the preacher closed in prayer, Jim was baffled. The man had only read one verse from the Bible, then told a story that had nothing to do with the Scripture he had read. Jim wondered if he'd pirated the whole anecdote from *Reader's Digest.*

After the service, Jim stood in line to greet the pastor. 'Oh, you're new!' he said and slapped Jim on the shoulder. 'Why don't you come to a study group I'm teaching later today.'

'Sure,' Jim said. 'I'd love to.'

That afternoon he found himself in a room with an eclectic group of people. Before the pastor could open the conversation Jim raised his hand.

'Yes. You're name's Jim, right?' the pastor asked. 'Do you have a question?'

Jim nodded. 'Recently, I have heard a lot about "being saved". I was wondering what someone should do to be saved.'

The pastor smiled and surveyed the room. He waved his hand in invitation and said, 'Go ahead anyone. Who wants to answer Jim's question?'

Jim looked around, but no one would meet his eye. Everyone found something very interesting to study on the floor. After an uncomfortable silence the pastor cleared his throat. 'That's a good question Jim. And, ah, you've come to the right place.'

THE TRUTH THAT TRANSFORMED ME

He gave a gesture that encompassed the room. 'The first thing you must do is join a group like this.' He smiled benevolently at each person. Everyone glanced up at the preacher and returned his smile. 'You must go to church every Sunday,' the pastor continued.

Jim noticed the man next to him square his shoulders.

'And,' the pastor raised his index finger and pointed up, 'try to be a better person.'

Everyone murmured agreement and a couple of people applauded. The pastor grinned and waved both hands palms down as if to say, 'No, don't clap. I'm glad we are in agreement.'

Jim frowned. He raised his hand again and said, 'But I heard a preacher on the radio say that Jesus is –.'

The pastor raised a defensive hand and cut Jim off saying, 'Let's save those questions for later, okay? What we came here to do this afternoon is get to know each other. Jane,' he said to the girl on his left, 'why don't we start with you?'

Jim tapped his foot and crossed his arms waiting for the hour to creep by. When everyone stood to leave he bee-lined to the pastor.

'Excuse me, sir,' Jim said. 'I have another question I would like to ask you.'

The pastor turned toward Jim and stuck out his right hand. When Jim took it in a handshake the pastor said, 'Thank you for coming, why don't you call my secretary this week and make an appointment. Good-bye.'

Jim watched the man retreat and whispered under his breath, 'He hasn't the foggiest idea how to know God any more than I did two days ago.'

That week Jim made a few phone calls and found his high school band director had moved to a different church, a Presbyterian church a few blocks from Jim's apartment. The next Sunday Jim tried this new church.

After the service a young man about his age grasped Jim's hand. 'You're new here aren't you?' he asked.

'Yes,' Jim said as he shook the fellow's hand.

'Name's Bob. What's yours?

'Jim.'

'Well, Jim, why don't you come to our Bible study tonight? It's for guys and girls our age. It's great. You could get to know some folks in the church.' With every sentence Bob pumped Jim's hand up and down as if shifting gears in a sports car.

Jim stepped back in an effort to extract his hand. 'I don't think so. I'm pretty busy,' he said, remembering last Sunday's fiasco at the other church.

Bob stepped forward and continued his invitation in a staccato burst of speech, 'Come on! You'll love it. Just try it.'

Jim pulled his hand again, but the guy wouldn't let go.

'It's tonight. Six-thirty. At the church.' Bob jacked Jim's hand up and down emphasizing each phrase.

'Okay!' Jim said jerking his hand away. The young man released it and Jim stumbled backward.

'You'll be here?' Bob asked.

'Yes. Six-thirty?' Jim asked as he massaged his fingers to help the blood return its flow.

'See you tonight?' Bob reached out to shake Jim's hand again.

Jim stepped back and gave a wave instead. 'Yeah, tonight.'

'Bring your Bible,' Bob called over his shoulder as he turned to go.

'Bible?' Jim said with a crack in his voice that rivaled a pubescent teen.

Bob stopped and turned around. 'Yeah! You know, it's a Bible study.' He pronounced the words Bible and study slowly as if explaining a difficult concept to a small child.

'Oh, right!' Jim called. He gestured with his hand as if to say, I knew that. He turned around and frowned to himself. 'Bible? Where am I going to find a Bible?'

When he returned to his apartment, Jim opened the hall closet. Skis, life belt, his old boxing gloves, and a various assortment of sports equipment crashed down upon him. He made an effort to catch the avalanche but failed. As he picked up the long skis to prop them back up he upset a box of ping pong balls. They tick-tocked off the hardwood floor and ricocheted off the walls in every direction.

He squinted up afraid something else might crash down on him, and found what he was looking for. A battered cardboard box sat on the top shelf next to his black clarinet case.

'Sorry, old pal,' Jim said as he shoved the clarinet to the side and grabbed the box.

The lid was coated with a thick layer of dust. A ray of sunlight gleamed down on it. Motes drifted lazily in the beam. He felt like Jim Hawkins in *Treasure Island* when he found the pirate's trove. With great expectations, he carefully lifted the top. What he saw inside took him back ten years.

He pulled out a golden trophy with a football player cradling a golden ball under one arm and holding the other straight out as if blocking opponents. He smiled, remembering his brief glory as the quarterback in Chicago. There were several smaller awards he had earned in music along with his Boy Scout sash covered with the badges. He had forgotten he packed these treasures when he'd left his parents' home. Something red lay at the bottom of the box. It was partially covered with other papers, but he knew what it was. It was the reason he had searched for the box in the first place. He laid aside all his awards and medals and reached down into the bottom of the box to lift it out.

The item was stiff and creaked in complaint when he opened it. Its pages stuck together and he had to lick his fingers to separate them. He turned to the second page, stood up and walked to the lounge chair in his living room. He clicked on the lamp on the end table and leaned back.

'Genesis, Exodus, Leviticus, Numbers,' he read. Then he closed his eyes and recited, 'Genesis, Exodus, Levit, Leviti –.' He opened his eyes. 'Cuss Leviticus, I guess that's how you say it. Leviticus, I didn't realize the Bible had cuss words.' He laughed to himself. Then he began to memorize all the books in the Bible.

After a bit he could recite them all, Old Testament and New. *They can't laugh at me now if they ask me to read something. I know where to find it.* He closed the Bible with a satisfied sigh.

'Matthew, Mark, Luke and John,' he sang as he brushed his teeth and got ready to go.

He attended the study every week, and pored over his notes, relishing the Biblical text. The most exciting words he'd ever read jumped off the pages as if alive, kindling a fire in his heart. Because he studied the lessons diligently Jim was the most prepared student in the group. After a few weeks the Bible study leader made an announcement. 'This will be my last night to meet with you. I've been offered a promotion at work, but it requires I move to another city.' He turned to Jim with a smile and said, 'Jim, you know a lot about the Bible. Why don't you take over leading this study?'

9

COMPETING FOR CHRIST

Soon after Jim knelt in his living room to receive Christ as Savior, he won the Tampa area Arthur Murray dance competition. He traveled to Jacksonville for the state competition and danced his way into the winner's circle.

After Jim walked away with first prize at the regional contest in Nashville, he boarded a plane for New York City. Thousands of instructors across America had vied for a spot at the Olympiad of dancers in the Big Apple. As soon as Jim arrived at Arthur Murray's famous studio on 5th Avenue he considered taking off his shoes, for this place was hallowed ground to the dance world. It was where Arthur Murray produced his weekly T.V. show, 'Arthur Murray's Dance Party,' for CBS.

In the large ballroom, mirrors lined the walls reflecting his image a thousand times in their depths. He grinned and waved. His reflections returned the compliment.

'Hello there, Mr. –,' a voice behind Jim began.

Jim spun around. 'Mr. Murray!' he exclaimed, throwing out his right hand.

'How 'bout that. I'm Mr. Murray, too,' Arthur Murray smiled as he shook Jim's hand.

'No, I'm Kennedy. Jim Kennedy,' Jim said with a laugh. He gestured helplessly with his left hand, 'I was just so surprised to see –.'

'Why didn't you say so, young man?' Mr. Murray interrupted. He clapped Jim on the back. 'Jim Kennedy. I saw your name on the list. Let's see now.' Arthur Murray closed his eyes as if trying to remember. 'You won our southeast competition. Right?' He grinned at Jim.

'Yes sir,' Jim said taking a deep breath and throwing his shoulders back.

'Why don't you come meet the rest of our contestants,' Mr. Murray said, and motioned for Jim to follow him into an adjacent room.

Ohh, Jim groaned inwardly when he saw the northeast, midwest and west coast competition winners. He recognized one of the fellows. He was famous, practically a household name. *I'll never beat him*, Jim thought.

When Jim went to his hotel room that evening, he knelt by his bed and prayed. 'Lord, help me to win this contest. Be with me as I dance and as they interview me on my salesmanship. Give me the right words to say.'

After each segment of the competition, Jim ran back to his room and repeated his prayer. He had to perform several complicated dances as well as show his proficiency as a salesman.

At the finish, Jim stood with the other contestants, breathing hard after his final competition and waiting for the results to be announced. Jim waited nervously, shifting his weight from foot to foot. He glanced at the other dancers. They each looked so cool and confident. He shifted his shoulders back and breathed long deep breaths to calm his nerves.

Anne had traveled to New York to watch him in the final contest. She stood at the edge of the room with her arms crossed, along with the fingers of each hand.

Arthur Murray read the results. 'And the winner of the 1952 Arthur Murray All-American Dance Competition is none other than ...' dramatic pause and drum roll. 'Jim Kennedy of Tampa, Florida!'

Jim's jaw dropped. He couldn't believe it. He looked at his competitors then looked at Anne. She clapped wildly, jumping up and down.

Arthur Murray and Mrs. Murray walked onto the dance floor to congratulate him. Camera lights flashed and popped, capturing the moment. Jim blinked and smiled. 'Thank you, thank you,' he responded to the Murrays' and other contestants' accolades.

Jim couldn't stop grinning. He was bursting to tell someone why he won the contest. He grabbed his dancing coach by the sleeve. 'The only reason I won was because I prayed. God made me win,' he said, his voice hushed in awe.

His coach's face was a calm pool where Jim saw clearly reflected that he thought his young pupil had gone off his rocker. He smiled awkwardly and patted Jim's arm as if calming a lunatic on the fringe. 'Yes, I see. Well. Good job.' He turned and quickly walked away glancing back once over his shoulder.

Jim laughed to himself as his coach retreated, then he ran to Anne. 'I knew you'd win!' she said throwing her arms around him in a tight hug. 'I'm so proud of you.'

Jim's win brought him instant notoriety. At age twenty-two he was chosen to serve on the prestigious National Dance Board, a group of mentors responsible for creating and formulating new dance steps for all the Arthur Murray studios around the country.

Jim had the world by the tail. His masculine good looks, lithe body, impeccable dress and manners required by the Arthur Murray program, attracted people to him. When news spread of his dancing fame, he was inundated by requests from various church groups to give his testimony.

He asked Anne to accompany him to his first meeting. She was surprised that this man who had never gone to church was going to speak to a religious youth group. Out of curiosity she accompanied him one Saturday night.

After the meeting Jim drove Anne back to her home in Lakeland. 'You sure are quiet,' he said, glancing at her out of the corner of his eye. 'What's the matter? Didn't you like the meeting?'

Anne sat rigid with her arms crossed tightly in a defensive manner. 'It was fine,' she snapped.

'What's wrong, Anne?'

'Nothing.'

'Nothing?'

'Don't repeat everything I say like an echo in the Swiss Mountains. I said, "Nothing's wrong." I just don't see why you had to make such a fool of yourself at the meeting tonight.'

'Make a fool of myself?'

'Echo. Do I hear an echo,' she said, cupping a hand behind her ear. 'I can't believe you told those impressionable young people to come forward if they wanted to accept Jesus as their Savior.'

'What?' Jim asked. 'Why would you be upset at me asking people to come to Christ? Don't you think it's important?'

'Who are you to lecture me on God?' Anne stared daggers at Jim. 'I've been going to church all my life. I think I know a little bit more than you do, mister!'

'I-I didn't say you didn't,' Jim stammered.

They drove the rest of the way home in silence. Anne jumped out of the car before Jim could open her door. 'Wait, Anne,' he said, 'Can I pick you up to go to the beach tomorrow.'

Anne slammed the door and called without turning back. 'Fine!'

Jim shook his head as he watched her go. 'I thought she'd be glad I became a Christian,' he mumbled to himself as he drove away.

The next day as they lay on towels soaking up the sun, Jim asked, 'Anne, what must you do to be saved?'

She turned toward him and lifted her sunglasses as if checking to make sure it was still the same guy beside her. She replaced her glasses, but he could see her eyebrows arch above the dark lenses as she recited as if by rote, 'Believe on the Lord Jesus Christ and you shall be saved.' She smiled with only one side of her mouth and he wasn't sure if she was glad she answered correctly or thought he had sunstroke.

'Yes,' said Jim. 'I finally understood that fact not long ago. But, if you were to die and God asked, "Why should I let you into heaven?" What would you say?'

This time Anne's brow creased in a worry line. 'Well, I've gone to church all my life. I've hardly ever missed a Sunday. I've been very moral and I hardly ever sin. I tithe and I try to help people who are in need, and I –.'

'Whoa!' Jim held his hands up as if to stop a moving car. 'All I hear is I, I, I. You haven't said anything about Jesus.'

Anne jerked the sunglasses off her face and scowled. 'I'm a better Christian than you'll ever be. Why you just started going to church. You said,' she lowered her voice to mimic his deep tone, "I can be just as good a Christian if I don't go to church."' She replaced her sunglasses and crossed her arms defensively.

'I was wrong. In fact when you told me I couldn't be as good a Christian if I didn't go to church, it got me thinking. I listened to a pastor on the radio and he asked the same question, "If you died tonight, how do you know you'd go to heaven?" It really made me think, so I got this book and read all about how Jesus died for me and rose from the dead. I asked him to forgive me and be my Savior. Then I started going to church. I've even started teaching Sunday school.'

The glasses came off again. He saw the whites of her eyes wide around the deep blue iris. Her mouth formed an O of unbelief. 'You! Teaching Sunday School? Why you've never been to church in your life.'

'I'm not talking about me, Anne. I'm talking about you. Do you know for sure that you are going to Heaven?'

'Don't you lecture me, Jim Kennedy!' she said shrilly. Jim glanced nervously to his left and right. He held his hands up again in a placating gesture. 'Sh, Anne. Do you want everybody on the beach to hear us argue?' He chuckled nervously and reached for her hand.

'Don't touch me Jim Kennedy,' Anne said in a huff. She stood and snatched up her towel, spraying Jim with a shower of sand.

10

CHANGE OF HEART

The next week Jim phoned. 'Anne, I'm speaking at a Youth for Christ rally tonight. Please come with me. I'm going to give my testimony. I want you to hear it.'

Silence.

He pressed on. 'I'd love to have you there. You can critique my speech.'

'Well, I can give you constructive criticism. I'm sure no one else would tell the truth to your face.'

He stared at the receiver as if it had bit his ear. 'Uh, that's great,' he said with a hollow laugh. 'Don't be shy, now. Why don't you say what you really think.'

Later that night, as Jim pulled into a parking spot at the conference center, he turned to Anne. 'Hey, I've got a great idea. Why don't you give your testimony? You can tell the kids what growing up in church has meant to you.'

Anne reached up and pushed the button down to lock her door. 'I refuse to get out of this car,' she said, and folded her arms tight across her chest. 'You can't make me stand in front of that group of people and make a fool of myself.' Her teeth came together with a sharp click.

'Oh, come on Anne. You'll be great. They'll love hearing from you.'

With one hand Anne grabbed the armrest of the door as if he would pry it out of her fingers and force her out. She stuck out her chin and shook her head in an adamant, No!

'Okay, I'm sorry.' Jim held out his hand. 'Just come on in. Please. I promise I won't say a word about you. I'll pretend I don't know you.'

She glared at him.

'I mean I will pretend I do know you. I mean. Ugh!' he sighed. 'You know what I mean. I won't call on you.'

At the meeting that night a young girl gave her testimony. She spoke of her ministry in India and her personal relationship with God through Jesus Christ.

Jim glanced at Anne. She stared up at the girl, her mouth slightly open as if drinking in the words.

When it was over Anne was silent, but not in the hard steely way she had been the week before. It was almost as if she had been deflated. In a kind of trance she walked to the car, then slumped into the passenger seat and stared at her hands in her lap.

Jim was afraid to ask what was wrong. He waited silently for her to respond. Finally, she turned to him, her blue eyes brimming. 'That girl has something I don't have,' she said in a small voice. 'I want what she has. I want to know God like she does. I've been to church all my life, but I've never really understood that knowing God isn't just a religion. It's a relationship with God through Jesus.'

Jim clenched his fists and said, 'Yes! Yes, that's just how I felt. Isn't it amazing!'

Anne looked up at him with pleading eyes. 'What do I do? Tell me. How do I get that kind of relationship she was talking about.'

Jim reached over and grasped her hands. 'Just ask,' he said and laughed. He threw a hand up and pointed to the sky. 'Prayer is just talking to God. We can pray right here, right now in this car, and God will hear us.'

He wrapped his arm around her shoulders. 'Pray with me. Lord Jesus,' he paused.

'Lord Jesus,' Anne repeated.

'I need you.'

'I need you.'

'Thank you for dying on the cross for my sins.'

'Thank you for dying on the cross for my sins.'

Anne spoke each phrase after Jim. 'Come into my life and be my Savior and Lord. I want to know you and have a personal relationship with you. Thank you for hearing me and coming into my heart. In Jesus' name. Amen.'

11

APRIL FOOLS

'Hey, Mr. Dance America.'

Jim looked up to see his old pal Billy standing in his office. He pointed at Jim's door and whistled. 'Manager! You're moving on up in the world. Why would you be going back to college?'

'Hey, Billy! I thought I'd better finish my education after all.' Jim wadded up a piece of paper and tossed it good-naturedly at his friend's head.

Billy grabbed it out of the air and straightened it out. 'Hey,' he said. His eyebrows shot up and he stared at Jim as if he'd changed colors. 'This is a flyer for the Youth for Christ rally. It says you are giving your testimony.'

'Yeah!' Jim said motioning Billy toward him. 'I've got to tell you. The most amazing thing happened to me. I became a Christian.'

'Wh-What?'

'Billy? Billy! Are you okay?' Jim stood up when his friend stumbled backward. 'Get off the floor. Come on. Don't act so surprised.'

'I-I-I am surprised, Jim. I became a Christian too.'

'Really? When?'

'About a year ago.'

'A year?' Jim's voice rose with incredulity. 'Why didn't you say anything to me about it?'

Billy rubbed his temple with his right hand. 'Wow, Jim,' he said haltingly. 'You were the last person in the world I thought would be interested in God. Remember when you decked that thug in the parking lot? I was scared you'd knock me out with one blow the same way.'

Jim raised his hand. 'Whoa, wait a minute. Your memory is a little skewed there buddy. That thug, as you say, was hassling an older gentleman. When I tried to intervene he took a swing at me.'

'I remember it perfectly,' Billy chimed in. 'You, Mr. Golden Gloves, dodged the villain's blow and returned it with a right jab of your own.'

'Yeah,' Jim laughed. 'I thought I whiffed the air. If you remember correctly I lost my balance and fell to my knees in front of the guy.'

'Is that what happened?' Billy asked, and laughed. 'I always wondered what happened. Man!' he shook his head in admiration. 'I'll never forget the look on that fellow's face as he collapsed on top of you.' Billy rolled his eyes up and acted as if he were fainting.

'Can you blame me for not telling you about Jesus? I was scared you'd clock me.' Billy held out a placating hand.

'Clock you? Are you crazy? For telling me how I could know God personally and be sure about going to heaven when I died?'

'Who told you then?'

'Donald Gray Barnhouse.'

'Who?'

'A radio preacher. He woke me up one morning and asked –.' Jim imitated Barnhouse's midwest tone. "If you died tonight and stood before God and He asked, 'Why should I let you into my heaven?' What would you say?"'

'Good question,' Billy said. 'What's the answer.'

'You should know if you're a Christian,' Jim chided. 'The only answer is that you've asked Jesus to pay for all your sins. No one is perfect and that's what God requires, perfection. That's why Jesus died. He lived a sinless life then died in our place. Because only someone completely faultless can pay the penalty for someone who has lied, cheated or sinned in any way. If they have done only one thing wrong, then they must pay for their own sin. So, the answer to the question, "Why should I let you into heaven?" is I have accepted the payment Jesus made on my behalf when He died on the cross. There is no other way to heaven or Jesus wouldn't have had to die.'

Billy whistled. 'Wow! You should be a preacher. That's the first time I really understood why Jesus really had to die.' He raised three fingers in the Boy Scout pledge. 'But I have invited Him into my heart. Really.'

'Funny you should say that,' Jim said, with a grin. 'I love studying my Bible and I've really enjoyed speaking at these Youth for Christ rallies. That's another reason I've gone back to college. Some day I may want to go to seminary.' 'I've started to feel funny working here at the dance studio.' He massaged the back of his neck and winced.

'Funny ha-ha or funny strange?' Billy asked.

'You know what I mean,' Jim said with a shrug. 'The other day a sailor came in for some lessons. He ogled one of the girls on the dance floor and elbowed me. "Boy, you sure are lucky."' Jim said, impersonating the sailor with a hillbilly twang. 'I'd give my right arm to be able to work in a joint like this.' Jim punched his right fist into his left palm. 'I wanted to knock him down the stairs.'

Billy backed up a step and raised his hands. 'Calm down, Jim. You have to know that's what all the guys think. This place does seem like the perfect pick-up joint. After all, didn't you meet Anne here?'

'Pick-up joint!' Jim said exploding out of his chair. 'That's contrary to all Arthur Murray's rules. This is a classy place, not some pick-up joint,' he said, spitting the words out like bitter seeds.

Jim sat back down, cradled his chin on his fists, and huffed. 'I know that's what people think. And I did meet Anne here.' He waved away the rumors. 'That's why I said it was funny that you said I should be a preacher. I'd love to preach, but Anne has said a thousand times, "I'll never marry a preacher."' He quoted Anne's words in a high-pitched tone. '"My sister married a preacher and now she lives in a fishbowl. All the parishioners scrutinize her every move."'

'Hmm,' Billy said sympathetically. 'Too bad.'

A tug of war raged in Jim's mind the next few weeks. Several incidents occurred that left him feeling more awkward about his profession. After lunching with a Christian Business Men's group, he went to pay for his meal. The cashier distractedly grabbed his check, keeping a constant smack as she blew and popped small pink bubbles. 'That'll be $4.35,' she said and glanced up quickly. When their eyes met her mouth dropped and the gum wad nearly tumbled from her lips into the cash register. 'It's you. Wow!' She craned her neck to look over his shoulder at the men behind him.

Jim turned to see what she was looking at. 'What's wrong?' he asked with a nervous laugh.

She leaned forward conspiratorially. 'I never thought I'd see *you* in a group like this.' She inclined her head toward the men behind him.

Jim leaned forward. 'Neither did I,' he whispered back with a grin.

She nodded and continued smacking the gum. 'See you later at –,' she gestured with her hands as if dancing 'you know where.' She held an index finger to her lips as if shushing a child. 'It'll be our secret.' She whispered with a wink.

Jim stared, momentarily bewildered. 'Uh, right.' He stepped back and gave a little wave.

The next Sunday he sat in church reading his Bible while waiting for the service to begin. As the organist began the prelude a trio of girls trooped down the center aisle in search of a seat. Suddenly the blonde in the lead stopped abruptly. The others, unaware traffic had stopped, rear-ended their friend in an undignified pileup. Along with the rest of the congregation, Jim glanced up to see what caused the wreck. A crimson burn inched up his neck when he saw a trembling finger point his way. 'He's my dance instructor. Look! He's in church!' the blonde whispered audibly behind a cupped hand to the two girls who had stumbled over her.

At the studio, Jim threw himself into his work, recruiting students and teaching classes. But, the nagging feeling that the dance studio was not where he belonged continued to bore into his heart.

In early December of 1955, he strode into his office, slamming and locking the door behind him. He stood for a moment panting and running his fingers through his hair. 'What should I do?' He looked up at the ceiling. 'Lord, what do you want from me?' He dropped onto his knees in front of his office chair, clasped his hands tightly and prayed, 'I'll do whatever you want me to do. Do you want me to quit?'

He jumped up and grabbed the phone to call in his resignation, then slammed it down and dropped to his knees again. 'How could you help me win the All-American Competition then want me to quit. I'm making such good money. With $750 a week I could get married and support a family. I could still give my testimony and teach Sunday school.'

He pressed his hands against his chest. 'Oh, my heart feels like you've got your fist around it! What do you want? Oh, Lord, tell me,' he shouted at the ceiling.

Jim stretched out full length onto the floor. His forehead pressed into the grit on the hardwood. He didn't even notice the dust that had accumulated in wads by the baseboards. He squeezed his eyes closed and groaned as he prayed. He was not sure how long he wrestled with God.

It seemed hours. Days.

But, he finally stood and threw back his shoulders. He clenched his jaw in determination as he spun the dial to phone his boss, the studio's owner.

'Hello?' came the voice at the other end of the line.

'Hey, Mr. Costello, it's Jim Kennedy.'

'Jim! Wow! What a coincidence. I was just about to pick up the phone and call you. I've got some news for you. You'll never believe it.'

'I've got some news, too,' Jim said, his voice a flat monotone.

'You've got to hear my news first.' John Costello continued, his voice animated with excitement. 'I want you to take over the Sarasota studio. Not as manager, but as –,' he paused dramatically, 'Can you guess! Come on, guess!'

'Uhh,' Jim said closing his eyes shaking his head as if his boss could see him. 'Mr. Costello, I've got to tell you.'

'Can't you guess? And you can't call me Mr. Costello. Partners have to be on a first-name basis. Partner, Jimmy boy, you hear me, owner of the new studio in Sarasota. Part-owner anyway, it'll be half yours and half mine. Do you realize what an incredible privilege this is? Your salary will double. Not just double – triple! You're on your way to early retirement. How old are you? Twenty-two, twenty-three?'

Jim stared at the receiver. 'Oh, Lord,' he moaned.

'Now Jim, don't be going religious on me. It's *me* you need to be thanking, not God,' he said with a laugh.

Jim looked up at the ceiling again and raised a hand as if pleading for help. He mouthed, 'Are you sure, God? Even now?'

'Jim? Jim? Have you passed out on the floor?' John Costello's laugh sounded distant through the phone line.

He's not going to be laughing long, Jim thought as he pinched the bridge of his nose between his finger tips. He inhaled deeply as if about to dive into deep water. 'Mr. Costello, I mean John, I called to tell you I'm resigning,' he said quickly, before blowing out his breath in a long sigh.

Silence.

'John. Mr. Costello.'

A cough then a chuckle sounded through the phone line. 'We must have a funny connection here, Jim. Is it windy there? Did you say, "Where am I signing?" I've got a contract right in front of me. I'll bring it over and you can sign it right away.'

Jim's legs felt weak. He sat down heavily in his chair and cradled his head in a hand. 'No, sir. I said I'm resigning.' Jim enunciated the word resigning with exaggerated clarity.

'Resigning?' his boss repeated. 'Resigning? What are you talking about? This is Jim Kennedy, winner of the Arthur Murray All-American and member of the prestigious dance board? You're joking. April fools, huh?'

'No, sir. It's no joke. I just don't believe this is the right place for me to be,' he cleared his throat, 'as a Christian, you know,' he added in a quiet tone.

'Christian? What are you talking about. Are you insinuating that I am not a Christian. That Christians can't work for Arthur Murray?'

'No! No, that's not what I mean. I just mean I think God is calling me to quit.'

Silence. Jim closed his eyes and waited for John Costello's response.

'Well,' he finally said breaking the pause. 'If that's how it is, Mr. Kennedy. I will have your replacement there on Monday morning.' Click.

'I was hoping I could work till the end of the month, till I could find something – Mr. Costello! Mr. Costello!' The dial tone buzzed in his ear and Jim glared at the receiver. He slammed it down then began to hammer his forehead with his fists in cadence to his words. 'What have I done?' Thud-thud-thud.

He raised his head and stared around his office. It was decorated with the accolades of his years at the studio. His photo with Mr. and Mrs. Arthur Murray after he won the All-American grinned down at him from the wall to his right. He jumped up and yanked it down, fished a box out from under his desk and threw it in.

After flinging in the rest of his personal effects he carried the box into the hallway.

'Mr. Kennedy?' a surprised voice sounded behind him.

Jim turned to face a young man he had recently recruited as an instructor.

'What-what are you doing?' the fellow asked gesturing at the box in Jim's hand.

Jim looked down morosely, then back into the empty office he had just vacated. 'I'm not sure,' he said truthfully.

'You're not sure?' the boy repeated. 'You don't know what you're doing?' he asked, stepping back and looking at Jim as if he were a mental patient escaped from an asylum.

Jim smiled and shook his head. 'I'm leaving. But I'm not sure where I'm going.'

'It's okay, Mr. Kennedy.' The new instructor held up a reassuring hand and backed away slowly. I'll get you some help.'

As Jim walked toward the stairway, he took a moment to glance around. He had been here six years. He had thought it was his ideal job. Jim swallowed hard, but the giant pill he just took was lodged in his ribcage and didn't go away. 'Lord, I'm going. Just show me where you want me,' he prayed under his breath as he descended the stairs.

12

OUT OF WORK

'Are you sure?' Jim said, practically choking with shock.

The teller sat smugly behind the iron bars and nodded her head. She pushed up her cat-eye glasses with an index finger. 'Yes, Mr. Kennedy. The bank doesn't make mistakes.'

Jim wondered if the bank required its employees to adopt a nasal tone when dealing with its customers.

'That seems impossible,' Jim said. He gripped the bars that separated him from the teller.

She pushed her glasses up again and arched a penciled brow. 'Well, sir,' she said in a pinched voice. 'I could read you the itemized list of expenditures you incurred since your last deposit.' Her brow rose even higher, deepening the creases on her forehead as she scanned the list.

'No, stop! I mean.' Jim coughed and glanced around. He said in a whisper, 'You don't have to read me my statement aloud. It is just hard to believe I have only thirteen dollars left in the bank.'

The teller stared blankly. She shrugged and gave a slight nod meaning, *Are you finished or not?*

Jim bumped his fists on the counter and lowered his eyes in defeat.

'Next!' the teller called around him.

He glanced behind him and stumbled sideways, then made his way to the door of the bank in a stupor. 'Where did the $750 a week go? How could I have spent all that money? What am I going to do for a job? How am I going to pay my rent? What am I going to tell Anne?' he muttered under his breath.

Not knowing where to turn next, Jim found himself driving to Hyde Park Presbyterian Church where he had attended since coming to Christ. He went in and knocked on the pastor's office door.

'Jim!' Dr. Campbell greeted him. 'Come in. My goodness, you're pale. Are you sick?'

Jim laughed mirthlessly and pressed his fist to his chest. 'I think I swallowed a lead weight,' he mumbled.

'Wait? Are you waiting for something?' the pastor asked.

'Yes,' Jim looked up with feverish eyes. 'I am waiting. I'm waiting on God to tell me what to do.' Jim recounted his last hours to the man of God who listened attentively, hands folded on his desk. He hm'd and ah'd at all the appropriate moments, nodding his head with what Jim hoped was approval. When Jim finished his story the pastor sat for a moment, his eyes staring up and lips pressed tightly together as if solving algebraic formulas in his head.

Jim held his breath hoping for a miraculous answer to his dilemma.

Dr. Campbell slapped his desk and Jim jumped. 'I've heard you've been doing a marvelous job in Sunday school.'

Jim nodded his head.

'Would you like to preach?' the pastor asked.

'*I'll never marry a preacher!*' Anne's words haunted Jim a moment before he answered.

'I think maybe that's what God is calling me to do,' he said, studying the pastor's face intently to make sure his question was sincere and not a joke.

Dr. Campbell spun a rolodex file of names and phone numbers next to the black telephone on his desk. He picked up a pair of reading glasses and focused on one of the cards. 'There's a little Presbyterian Church over in Clearwater,' he said glancing up at Jim over the half-glasses. Their pastor is due to retire in February.' He pointed at the card and said, 'Why don't I give him a call to say you'll deliver the sermon tomorrow morning.'

Mentally, Jim tabulated his expenses times the three months he would have to wait for the elderly pastor to retire. 'Sure,' he said, balling his fist and pushing his sternum in an effort to ease the pressure of the lead weight lodged against his heart.

After leaving Dr. Campbell's, Jim jumped in his car and raced to Lakeland. 'Anne, I know you said you'd never marry a pastor,' he said to the empty passenger seat. 'No, that's not right. You said you would never marry a minister. A preacher.' He cleared his throat, tilted his head slightly and began again. 'Anne, I've quit my job. No, that's wrong,' he muttered. 'Anne, I prayed and prayed and God impressed on me to quit my job.' The miles ticked by like seconds and Jim rehearsed his speech a thousand different ways.

When he arrived at her family's home, Anne burst out the front door as if she'd expected him. 'Jim!' she squealed and jumped into his arms.

'Anne!' He breathed in her perfume and clasped her in a tight embrace. 'I'm going to be a pastor. I quit my job. You've got to marry me because I love you.' His words tumbled out, wrecking his practiced speech.

'What? You do? Oh, Jim!' Anne kissed him hard on the lips.

'Does this mean you will? Even though you said you never would?' Jim asked, his voice a mixture of excitement and apprehension.

'I never said I wouldn't marry you! You never asked before. Of course I will.'

'No,' Jim shook his head with a tentative smile. 'You said you'd never marry a pastor. Did you hear me right? I quit my job today and I'm going to be a preacher. In fact I'm going to preach tomorrow.'

Anne squeezed him tighter, her eyes dancing with delight. 'I said that before I invited Jesus into my heart. Now that I truly know God, I can't think of anything I would rather do than serve Him at your side.'

'Anne,' Jim grabbed her shoulders and held her away from him, 'You've got to know, I'm broke. I only have thirteen dollars in the bank.'

Anne batted his hands away and wrapped her arms around him again. 'God has always provided for his people. I trust Him. And –,' she put her nose to his and stared him directly in the eyes. 'I trust you, too.'

Jim darted a glance at his watch. 'I think I can whip up a sermon in the next few hours.'

'Oh, Jim! Go! Go!' Anne jumped back and shooed him toward his car. 'Get busy. Prepare.'

'You'll come?' Jim asked as he folded behind the wheel.

'Wild horses couldn't keep me away,' Anne said, leaning through the car window, tickling him under the chin with her fingers.

Bethel Presbyterian Church in Clearwater could have been a historic landmark which had been built by stout Florida pioneers nearly eighty years before. Anne leaned forward to get a better view. 'It's sort of cute,' she said, craning her neck to see its roof line.

'Cute,' Jim said. 'That was number one on my list for a church.'

'Oh, hush,' she said, punching his shoulder. 'Just because you're nervous doesn't mean you have to be cynical.'

'It's a miniature castle. The tower above the door looks like some sort of a battlement. I can just see the parishioners lying in wait before they lean out the embrasures and shoot prospective pastors who preach poorly,' Jim said, feigning a nervous glance at the invisible archers as he opened Anne's car door.

Anne stifled a giggle as they walked hand-in-hand toward the white stone building. The Reverend greeted the young couple when they entered. In his long flowing robe and vestment, the elderly gentleman looked slightly out of place in the small country church. He shook Jim's hand formally, led him to a chair on the platform, then stood at the podium to perform the opening rituals for the small congregation.

Jim furtively glanced at his notes as the preacher droned on with the announcements. When he looked out at the congregation dressed in their Sunday best, his leg jittered with nerves. 'Lord,' he closed his eyes and silently prayed, 'how am I going to live on thirteen dollars for the next three months?' He pressed his fist into his sternum once again to dislodge the iron ball anxiety had deposited.

'You all know I have planned to retire in February,' the robed clergyman said to the crowd. Jim pricked up his ears. It was almost time for him to stand and deliver. 'However,' the pastor said and paused, fixing his gaze on the people over the top of his gold pince-nez, 'since the board has sent this nice young man over to preach this morning –,' he directed a spacious gesture in Jim's direction, 'I've decided to retire immediately. So I want you to join me in welcoming your new pastor. Jim, come on up here.'

The congregation stared in unblinking expectation as Jim stood and shook their former pastor's hand. He turned toward the crowd seated in the pews, gulped twice, then cleared his throat. 'Thank you, sir,' he said, and clutched both sides of the podium to anchor himself.

At that moment his Arthur Murray training kicked in. This was no different than giving his presentation in New York at the dance competition. He raised his right hand and said, 'Turn in your Bibles to the twenty-second chapter of Matthew.' As he flipped the pages, his heart leapt and he realized the weight of anxiety was gone. He had a job. He could pay his rent. He wouldn't starve the next three months. God had met his needs. He wanted to shout. He wanted to sing. He wanted to dance.

As he started preaching his feet began to move. He stepped to the side then together, kicked a toe back then forward, and unconsciously hoofed the latest steps he had developed for the national dance board. His body remained rigid, almost, but his feet took on a life of their own.

Jim didn't notice, but Anne told him later the congregation hardly listened to a word he said. They all watched their former pastor watch Jim's footwork. The minister's eyebrows shot up then wrinkled together like a fuzzy white caterpillar. His facial expressions were enough to make Anne have to cover her mouth to keep Jim from seeing her laugh.

At the end of the service the minister rose, cold as an iceberg. He fixed Jim with a patriarchal glare before gliding to the back of the church to shake hands with the members of his former congregation.

On their drive back to town Jim couldn't quit grinning. 'Anne,' he said, giving her hand a squeeze. 'Do you realize in the last twenty-four hours I quit my job, got engaged, and became a preacher.'

Anne squeezed back. 'Do you realize it hasn't even been a year since you've become a Christian?'

Jim laughed. 'I am amazed. I don't think I've ever really known true joy before receiving Christ. Did I tell you it felt like I swallowed an iron ball after quitting my job and finding out I only had thirteen dollars in the bank?'

Anne shook her head. 'Are you okay?' she asked with concern in her voice.

'Yes! It's gone. Gone!' Jim punched the air. 'God is amazing isn't he.'

'Yes, darling,' Anne laughed. 'He is. But watch out...!' She flung up a hand pointing to the curve in the road.

Jim jerked the wheel back onto the pavement when the gravel on the shoulder of the road spattered the undercarriage. 'We're okay. Don't worry about anything,' he said. 'I'll never worry again. I've seen that where God guides, God provides. Although I will have to tighten my belt a bit.'

'Tighten your belt?' Anne asked.

'Did I mention how much the church pays their illustrious pastor?'

Anne shook her head.

'Two-hundred-fifty dollars a month.' He made a quick mental calculation. 'I'm taking a pay cut from my former salary of approximately $2,750 a month.' He cut his eyes over, quickly glancing at Anne. 'Are you sure you still want to marry me?'

'I've never seen you happier, Jim. Money can't buy joy. I'd rather be poor and happy than rich and miserable.'

Jim stared at Anne's earnest face. 'Come here!' he said, reaching his arm out for her to snuggle in closer. 'You are the most amazing woman in the world.'

There were a lot of loose ends to tie up at the studio and Jim came the next week to meet his replacement. A middle-aged woman, who had been one of his students, met him in the ballroom.

'Is it true, Jim?' she asked, arresting him with an outstretched arm.

Jim stepped back and tilted his head to one side. 'Ma'am?' he said, raising his brows.

'Is it true,' the woman said in a officious tone, 'that you are leaving this work and plan to go into the ministry?'

'I'm not planning on it,' Jim said with a half smile. 'I'm in it already.'

The woman raised her brows. 'My, that was quick. I can't imagine who will be able to take your place here.' She looked around her with a disdainful glance. 'You were by far the best instructor. Quite famous too. Hmm,' she said with an air of disappointment.

'Promise me one thing, Jim,' she said suddenly brightening.

'Yes, ma'am,' Jim said, wondering what in the world she could want him to do.

'I have a good friend you should talk to before you leave. He is a respected doctor and I think he will give you some important insights that you need to hear. Promise me you'll go,' she demanded.

Jim nodded with a frown. 'Yes, ma'am. If you want me to.'

'You should want to for yourself, Jim.' The woman pulled a business card from her handbag and passed it to him. I'll call and tell him to expect you.'

Jim looked at the card and immediately regretted his promise. He glanced up and watched the woman descend the stairs. One of the instructors approached him and whistled a soft whoo. 'She is strange. What did she want?'

Jim held up the card and the fellow took it. 'This address is in old town. What is it?'

'She wants me to go and visit her doctor friend,' Jim said in a sarcastic tone.

'I've seen her friends,' the instructor said and shuddered. 'Weird.'

'That's putting it kindly,' Jim said taking the card back.

'Good luck.'

'Thanks, I'll need it.'

Jim drove through the old neighborhood where large old live-oaks stretched wide their crooked arms, shadowing the street from the bright sun above. The doctor's office was located in his rambling gloomy home. As Jim made his way up the sidewalk he noticed the windows were shrouded with heavy drapes. He expected Lurch, the butler on 'The Addam's Family' TV show, to greet him when he rang the bell. Instead, a diminutive woman escorted Jim in. He stood in the entrance taking in the flavor of the old home. It wasn't any cheerier on the inside. The large overstuffed furniture gave him the creeps. He shuddered.

When Jim heard a door close he turned to see a gaunt gentleman with a sepulchral expression shuffle toward him. Jim took a deep breath and said a quick prayer to prevent himself from running out the door. *I think I've stepped into a Hollywood horror movie,* he thought. But he forced his arm up and gave a slight wave. 'Hello,' Jim said in a croaking voice. He covered his mouth and cleared his throat. 'I'm Jim Kennedy.'

The gaunt man, dressed in funereal black, scanned Jim up and down with his watery eyes. 'Young man,' he intoned in a low voice, 'I understand you are going into the ministry.' He spoke the last word as if he'd bitten down on a lemon.

'Yes, sir. That is correct.' Jim shifted his weight and stuck his hands deep into his pockets.

'Young man,' the doctor said, seeming to find Jim's youth a sticking point, 'people need more than to be talked at,' he said pointedly. He pivoted, turning his back on Jim, and returned to the recesses of his house. Jim heard a door slam and jumped.

He looked around but the woman who had let him in was gone too. 'Whoa,' he said to the empty room and stared around with a frown. 'That was weird,' he whispered under his breath.

As he walked back to his car he tried to pray. 'What was up with that, Lord?' He shook his head and said to himself, 'If people don't need to be "talked at," could the doctor be right? Is there really a need for preachers?'

13

INSULTS AND MOSQUITOES

'I have something I want to give you,' Jim said when he picked Anne up at her home in his Pontiac. 'Let's drive down to Lake Hollingsworth. You still have to do a water-ski show for me. I wish I could have watched your ballet on the long boards.'

'I miss those long days in the sun and the smell of petrol as it smoked from the engines on Dad's patched-up boats. Our old barn where he used to practice veterinary medicine is now full of boats he's either in the middle of building or given up on.' Anne looked longingly at the glassy lake. 'I wish I could make a living in my bathing suit instead of skirts and nylons. I'm sick of working in that office. I'd like to tell my boss just what I really think of him. It would be constructive criticism.'

'I'm sure it would,' Jim said with a laugh.

'Really!' Anne elbowed him. 'Don't laugh. I think it would do him some good.'

Jim pulled the car up to the dock and switched off the engine. They both sat for a moment, each silently brooding on private dreams as the setting sun painted the water orange and red with its dying beams. Jim turned to Anne and took her left hand in his. 'I think I love you more now than I've ever loved you. I want to shout to the world how wonderful you are and that you belong to me.'

He looked down at her fingers and gave them a gentle squeeze. 'There's just something not quite right about this hand of yours. But I think I have something that will remedy the situation.' He fumbled in his pocket for a moment then slipped something cool and round onto her fourth finger. 'Now I can officially ask you to marry me.'

Anne stared at the sparkling diamond. 'Oh, Jim!' she said breathlessly. When she looked at him with glistening eyes, his heart seemed to grow three sizes. 'It is exquisite. You have such good taste! How could you afford it?'

'The studio sent me a check for three hundred dollars. They said it was a belated Christmas bonus. Isn't God good?'

'God has blessed you more and more since you committed your life to Him. I can't wait to see all He will do in our lives.'

Jim spent the next months pulling up his grade point at Tampa University from the C average he earned before his hiatus from the halls of learning. He began racking up A's and B's on his papers and exams and passed many days in the library researching seminaries. The closest Presbyterian seminary was seven miles east of downtown Atlanta, Georgia. But his initial interest in Columbia stemmed from a printed sermon he came across in one of the school's catalogs. Dr. Cecil Thompson, professor of evangelism at Columbia, wrote a plea that emphasized the necessity of preaching the gospel to bring lost souls to Christ. 'Too many sermons,' the professor argued, 'were not drawing the needed response from congregations. Those who delivered such sermons might as well be firing a machine gun into a mud bank.' This was the kind of teacher Jim was looking for and his choice was made.

When he was not working to fulfill his English degree, Jim memorized large passages of Scripture in preparation for Sunday sermons at Bethel Presbyterian.

Anne spent her spare time in Lakeland preparing for their wedding which would take place on August 25. Almost every weekend she trekked to Clearwater to hear Jim preach. She was still his best critic and he valued her input. However, she wasn't the only one.

Jim never tired of calling his new congregation to surrender their lives completely to Christ. He didn't want to 'fire the machine gun into the mud bank' by leaving out the gospel. Each Sunday he worked the Good News into the message and it wasn't long before someone let him know what they thought about his altar calls.

After church, Jim stood in the back shaking hands and greeting each person as they exited. A white-haired gentleman came up behind him and grabbed his elbow. Jim turned with a smile and held out his right hand to the man he recognized as one of the church elders.

'Good morning Mr. –' he began, but faltered when the man grimaced at the gesture as if Jim handed him a rotting fish. He squinted up at Jim shortsightedly. 'Young man,' he said with a sniff, 'why do you persist in cramming Jesus down our throats every Sunday?'

Jim stepped back as if the man had struck him. 'Sir,' he said, 'I am only preaching what the Bible says. It's not I, but God who says that Jesus is the only way to heaven.'

The man narrowed his eyes and furrowed his brows. 'Young man,' he said, emphasizing the word young, 'we prefer our clergy to be well-educated.' Then abruptly, he spun on his heel and stalked away. Jim watched as the elder's wife tried to overtake him. She reached for his arm and made an effort to speak, but he jerked away, hunched his shoulders and pressed on like a running back through the defensive line.

Anne laid her hand gently on Jim's forearm. It was still outstretched to shake the elder's hand. 'It's okay, darling,' she said, looking up at him with a smile. 'Insults are like mosquitoes to a farmer; they should be expected and endured but most of all ignored.' She directed him back to the few people who stood waiting to shake his hand.

Next in line was Mrs. Barnum, the diminutive woman who played the piano. 'Oh, my,' she said, laying wrinkled fingers over her mouth. 'I am so sorry, Mr. Kennedy. I hope you won't get a bad impression of us here at Bethel because of that man.' She punctuated *that man* with a scowl in the direction the elder had retreated. Suddenly, her face brightened as though a light bulb blinked on behind her translucent skin. 'You know, I don't live far from here.' She turned and motioned with her small black purse. 'My house is right down that street. Why don't you come by this Wednesday and I'll invite some of our little flock over to meet you in person. You can give us a little message and say a little prayer or something. We can have a little coffee or something special.'

Anne covered her mouth and turned her head to hide her smile from the little lady to whom everything seemed to come in small packages.

'Oh!' the woman gasped, 'My dear! How did you smash all of your fingers at once? Your nails are –' the woman practically swooned, and Jim grabbed her arm to prevent her from toppling backward.

Anne's eyes went round as she stared at Mrs. Barnum in surprise. She held her hands palm down to examine them. 'Oh, my!' she laughed, then took a deep breath to sober her countenance. 'It's all right. Really.' Anne reached toward the woman who looked as if she wanted to recoil from Anne's hand but felt sympathy for her at the same time.

Anne held her fingers for the woman to see. 'I'm sorry I frightened you. It's my nail polish. I love all the colors of the rainbow.'

A smile flitted across the woman's lips as if she vacillated between relief and shock. 'But my dear,' she said laying a blue-veined hand over her heart. 'Black is not a color in the rainbow.'

Anne looked at her nails. 'You are so right,' she said earnestly. 'Besides, black doesn't go with my new diamond anyway.'

'How right you are, dear,' the old lady said. She grasped Anne's hand and squeezed.

'Green maybe or blue,' Anne said, glancing up and tapping her finger against her chin pretending to consider.

'Green?' the elderly lady said with a squeak.

'I'm teasing,' she said. 'You are so kind to offer Jim your home on Wednesdays. I hope I can come from Lakeland for the Wednesday night meetings too.'

'Oh yes, dear. You must. A wife should always support her husband,' Mrs. Barnum said with a twinkle in her faded blue eyes.

The prayer group which met at Mrs. Barnum's house not only built Jim's confidence as a young preacher, but also galvanized the members of the church in their walk with God. Jim didn't water down his sermons because one man disagreed but kept preaching the gospel, a fact for which deacon, Bill Kirkpatric, was grateful.

Jim wrote Anne in response to a letter she sent him from Lakeland. In her correspondence, she told him she had found courage to share her Christian testimony for the very first time. He also had some exciting news of his own.

Dearest, Dearest, Dearest, Dearest Anne,
Praise the Lord! I prayed that you would have the courage to give your testimony to someone this week. I prayed in my room then walked down stairs and read your letter. How wonderfully God answers prayer! I love you more than I have ever loved you before! I just want to go and tell

everyone how wonderful you are. Sharing your testimony is a big step, Anne, and you are bigger in my eyes than before.

It takes a big person to empty one's self and give all the credit to Christ. That's what Paul and Knox and Luther and Livingstone did. Now that you have 'come all the way out' for Christ, you will have power you never had before.

Expect some people to misunderstand – that's bound to happen – but keep looking up. I pray the Lord will let you see some conversions soon. Pray – and you'll have them.

Bill Kirkpatric, our deacon, raised his hand for salvation Tuesday. Mrs. Barnum and I prayed for him Monday night. Praise the Lord!

I feel like cords of steel bind us together now, Anne.

I love you completely,

Jim

14

THE RIVIERA

'Da dum de dum,' Jim hummed the wedding march as he buttoned his tuxedo. 'How do I look, George?' he asked spreading his arms and turning around.

'Like a million bucks,' George said and straightened Jim's bow tie. He brushed his little brother's shoulders with a sweep of his hand then turned him to look in the mirror. 'Does your face hurt yet?'

'Hurt?' Jim asked.

'Yeah. You know, from smiling so much.'

Jim massaged his jaw and opened and shut his mouth a few times. 'It still pops from where that sailor decked me.'

'Aw, quit your complaining. I fixed it better than any surgeon could – and for much less.'

Jim looked at his brother out of the corner of his eye and grinned. 'You know, George, I've just got to tell you about how Jesus has changed my life.'

George held up a hand. 'Jim, you have told me. Remember? You wrote me. I got it. I don't want to talk about it right now. Later. Let's not spoil your big day.'

'But George,' Jim began.

George glanced at his watch then turned for the door. 'Time to go.'

The music of the organ surged as Jim and his brother stepped into the sanctuary. Jim looked out at the crowded pews filled with new and old friends. Mrs. Barnum dabbed her eyes with a handkerchief clutched in white-gloved hands. Jim raised his chin in acknowledgment of his old buddy Billy's wave. His mom and dad sat stoically in the left front pew. His mother looked so happy and beautiful in her Sunday best. He saw a tear run down her cheek.

Jim focused his attention on the door at the back of the center aisle. Tension pulled at the pit of his stomach as if he sat at the top of the first hill of a roller coaster. He clamped his fingers into fists to hold tight. His Adam's apple bobbed up and down as he gulped.

George elbowed him. 'Calm down. You don't want to hurl.'

'I've never been so excited or nervous before,' Jim whispered out of the corner of his mouth. 'Even in New York at the All-American Dance Contest. This tops it all.'

'Here she comes. Look!' George nodded toward the aisle.

Jim's eyes went wide and his jaw slack. An angel clad in brilliant white stepped through the oak door. He vaguely wondered why Anne's father clutched the arm of the beauty who floated toward him to the tune of 'Here Comes the Bride.'

The wedding flew by in a haze of music and vows, but reality came into sharp focus when Jim heard the preacher announce, 'You may now kiss the bride.'

He exhaled a long breath and wondered momentarily if he had been holding it the whole service. Cupping Anne's face in his hands, he looked into her blue eyes and saw his love reflected there. He pressed his lips gently against hers and inhaled the fresh fragrance that clung to her hair.

Anne looked up at him and smiled, then grabbed his hand.

'Now may I introduce, Mr. and Mrs. Jim Kennedy,' the preacher said, and they walked out together as man and wife. During the reception, Jim kept glancing at his wristwatch as the minutes seemed to tick by slowly.

'Can we leave yet?' he whispered into Anne's frothy veil.

'Stop,' she said. 'You're pulling it off.' She reached up and adjusted the gauzy net that hung over her chocolate-brown coiffure. 'We have to greet our guests first.'

'We've greeted everyone. Let's go.'

A friend of Anne's came to give her a hug. 'Where are you two heading for your honeymoon?' she asked.

'Riviera Beach,' Anne said as she reached up and adjusted her veil for the hundredth time.

'Oo la, la. La Cote d'Azur! Parlez vous Francais?' the girl gushed.

'What?' Anne looked at her with a puzzled expression.

'La Cote d'Azur! The French Riviera. You must know if you're going there. Are you flying out tonight?'

'Oh, no!' Anne said. 'Not the French Riviera. The Riviera Beach in Florida!'

'You mean the Redneck Riviera,' her friend said with a scoffing laugh. 'That's not quite as romantic.'

'Oh, yes it is,' Anne said with a forced smile at this unbecoming remark. 'It doesn't matter where we go. If I'm with Jim it will be the most romantic place on earth.'

Rice rained down as they ran from the reception and jumped into Anne's car. Her father leaned in through the driver's window. 'I'll try to sell your car while you're gone, Jim. I've got a few ideas how to get good money for it.'

Jim reached up and shook his father-in-law's hand. 'Thank you, sir, and thank you for entrusting me with your treasure.' He glanced at Anne. 'We'll see you in a couple of weeks.'

'Jim?' Anne said as they drove away waving at their well wishers. 'Why is Dad selling your car?'

'We're going to eat it for the next year.'

'Eat your car?'

'Yummy! Lots of iron.'

'Jim! What are you talking about?'

'We're leaving for seminary in Atlanta when we get back from our honeymoon.'

'Yes, I realize that.'

'How else do you think we're going to pay for gas and food and a place to stay once we get there? I asked your dad to sell it so we could live on the proceeds next year.'

It took two days to drive to the most romantic beach on earth. The opalescent blue-green water sparkled jewel-like in its sandy white setting. Jim and Anne didn't lounge on the beach long before Jim began recounting a scuba trip he'd taken in the Bahamas.

'We left on a boat and went way out into the ocean,' Jim said as he lay on his side and twirled a lock of Anne's hair around his index finger. 'I had never been diving before, but the boat driver insisted there was nothing to it. They fitted me out with a weight belt to take me to the depths, and a tank, mask, fins, the whole works,' he said, sweeping his hand in a broad gesture. 'Then they pushed me out and said, "Just take deep breaths and have fun." As soon as I hit the water, the boat pulled away and left me to explore the reef on my own.'

Anne propped herself up on an elbow and faced Jim. 'They left you alone on your first dive?'

'They didn't go terribly far. I could still see them a good distance away. Anyway, I did exactly what they said. I put the regulator in my mouth and sucked in deeply.'

Anne gulped a deep breath in empathy. 'What happened?'

'Nothing.'

'What do you mean nothing?'

'No air.'

'Were you under water?'

'At first.'

'Did you come up for air.'

'No, you married a ghost. My body is at the bottom of the ocean somewhere south of here.'

Anne slapped his shoulder. 'Tell me what happened!'

'The weights were so heavy I had to work and work to keep my head above water. I kept sucking and sucking on the regulator, but I couldn't get anything. I thought, "Good grief, you must have to be some kind of Greek god to pull air up from those tanks." No matter how hard I tried I couldn't squeeze out one breath of oxygen.'

'What'd you do?'

'I swam and swam and swam. I thought I'd drown before I reached that stupid boat. I finally got close enough to hail them and they came to get me. When they pulled me out I told them I just wasn't cut out for this sport. After they stripped my tanks off and checked them they laughed.'

'They laughed at you? Why? Because you couldn't do it?'

'No,' Jim said. 'Evidently it wasn't so hard to breathe after all. The tanks they gave me had belonged to a man who died. They assumed they were filled with oxygen, but they were empty.'

'You mean the man who owned them died because he ran out of air? And you put your mouth on the same thing he did when he died!'

'He didn't die while he was diving. At least I don't think he did. Come to think of it –.'

'Well, did you ever get to go diving?' Anne interrupted.

'That is just the point I was coming to.' Jim thumped his hand on the sand. 'I did go diving, and they were right. It was easy. There's nothing like breathing under water! And I'm going to take you diving while we're here on our honeymoon, my love,' Jim said, scooping Anne into his arms and rolling her over. He kissed the tip of her nose. 'You'll love it,' he said. 'Trust me.'

That next day Jim and Anne rented diving equipment. They hiked onto a rocky jetty that reached out a long arm into the Atlantic.

'Why are we climbing over these boulders instead of taking the boat?' Anne asked as she delicately picked her way across Volkswagen size stones.

'Don't you remember my horror story? I don't want some boat to leave us stranded in the middle of the ocean on our second day of blissful union. Maybe after we've been married a few years and get tired of each other.'

'If I could pick up one of these rocks, I'd throw it at you, Jim Kennedy.'

'Now, Mrs. Kennedy. Is that any way to talk to your lord and master? Here we are. That wasn't too painful now, was it? Sit down and I'll help you put on your fins.'

'I think my feet are bleeding,' Anne said and propped a foot on her knee to inspect it.

'You're fine, stop complaining.' Jim put his hands on either side of her head and pulled her mask over her eyes. 'How does that feel? You look so cute when you're angry.'

'I'm not –.'

Jim stuffed the regulator between her teeth when she opened her mouth. 'Take a breath of that. Are you getting any air?'

'Uh, wah, wah, wunh,' Anne responded with a nod.

'I'll take that for a "Yes, my love."' Jim said and fitted his own mask over his face.

As they slipped into the water, Jim relaxed. He loved coming into this watery world. It was so quiet, and the light bent, bluing under the waves. He took Anne's hand and began to pull her out into open water.

Anne jerked her hand back. Jim swirled around to see what was wrong. She pointed at her goggles and tried to say something. Her regulator bubbled profusely, but Jim heard the tone of fear in her voice above the hiss and flow of air as it escaped into the silence of the water.

He swam close enough to see water sloshing inside her mask. It must have filled her nose because she appeared to be choking.

He knew she wouldn't be able to hear him, but made an effort to shout, 'Just breathe through your mouth.' He pointed to the regulator and made signs to convey what he couldn't say aloud.

All the while the heavy belt of weights kept pulling her deeper and deeper. Jim saw for the first time how huge the boulders of the jetty really were. They towered above them as they sank lower and lower.

Anne thrashed her arms and legs. She was panicking. He grabbed her hand and dragged her toward the surface. *I didn't want to go out in the boat because I thought that would be dangerous but here I am killing my wife anyway,* Jim thought as he kicked hard and fought his way back to the top.

'Relax! Just breathe through your mouth,' he yelled when they broke the surface. 'Let me help.'

Anne flailed her arms and spit out the mouthpiece. She gasped, 'I can't breathe!' A wave slapped her face and she choked.

'Relax! I'll take care of you. Remember, I'm a trained lifeguard.' Jim pulled her toward the jetty. As he treaded water while trying to adjust her mask, a large swell lifted the two of them before breaking on the rocks in a blanket of spray. When they dropped into the trough of the wave as it moved on through Jim shouted and winced in pain.

'What?' Anne asked, looking around wildly. 'Did something bite you.'

'My tailbone,' Jim said with a groan.

'Something bit your-your – bottom,' Anne said, and coughed up water when she started to laugh.

'It's not funny. And, no, something didn't bite my bottom. When the wave troughed I came down hard on the point of that boulder. I think I cracked my tail bone.'

'Oh, honey. I'm so sorry. It's all my fault. If I hadn't gotten my mask – I mean if I wasn't drowning – Well I guess I wasn't drowning. Come on, I'll help you. We can make it –.'

'I don't need any help. Are you fixed now?' Jim asked, cutting her off. 'I want to get as far away from this dumb rock as possible.'

Anne adjusted her mask, bit over the regulator, and put her face into the water to check for leaks, then put both thumbs up. The two submerged, leaving the roar and crash of waves for the quiet hiss and shush of their own breath as they explored the crystal blue water.

Later, when they lay exhausted upon the sand, Anne threw an arm over Jim. 'I loved it!' she said. 'Let's go again.'

Jim rolled on his side and winced.

'Are you okay?' she asked with a coo of sympathy.

'I will be. Oh! That smarts.'

'I guess we should have taken the boat,' Anne said with a shrug.

'Tired of me already.'

'Never, Anne said punctuating the word with a kiss.

15

STALACTITES IN THE TUB

A week after returning from the Riviera, Jim and Anne packed their worldly belongings and drove to Atlanta, Georgia. They bought an *Atlanta Constitution* newspaper and spent their first day in town checking out rentals near campus. The first place that caught their eye was listed as 'New garage apartment in Decatur. Low rent, good neighborhood.'

They drove around till they found the address, then sat in the car to assess the potential of the place.

'What do you think?' Jim asked.

'It's kind of cute,' Anne said.

'That's what you said about the church in Clearwater.'

'It was too. And look how well that turned out.'

'Do you think anyone is home?'

'We can always try.'

As Jim and Anne approached the three-car garage they saw a new stairway had been built on the left side. 'Do you feel it sway?' Anne asked as they climbed to the door at the top.

'Oh, that's just your imagination,' Jim said.

The door to the apartment was open. 'Anybody home?' Jim called and looked inside.

An elderly gentleman knelt on the opposite side of the room. He stood when he saw Jim and Anne at the door. 'Hi there,' he said and waved a wet paintbrush at them. A strong smell of varnish permeated the place. The man scratched his head then gestured at the circle of unvarnished floor. He laughed nervously. 'I think I've made a mess. But I guess I can't wait till it dries. I may starve.' He tiptoed to them, leaving footprints on his freshly finished floor. He looked down and frowned at his mishap, then shrugged. 'It'll buff out.' He waved the paintbrush into the doorway and grinned. 'Built it myself. It would be perfect for a newly-married couple.'

'How did you know we were newly married?' Anne asked with a note of surprise in her voice.

'I'm an old married man myself. I can always tell the new ones.'

Jim leaned in through the doorway and looked around the room. 'What do you think?' he asked Anne.

She bit her lower lip and looked around uncertainly, then gave a slow nod.

Jim threw out his arms and said, 'If you'll have us, we'll take it.'

It didn't take Anne long to land a job. One of the city's major brokerage houses hired her as an executive secretary. It provided them with a predictable family budget for Jim's three years of graduate study.

It didn't take Jim long to realize Columbia Theological Seminary wasn't the same school he had researched in the Tampa library. It had a remnant of professors who believed the Bible was the Word of God and the gospel it is dynamite to open blind eyes. Manfred George Gutzke was one of them. The ex-heavyweight boxing champ was still powerful in body but even more so spiritually. Jim laughed loud and often in Dr.

Gutzke's classes. He developed great respect and affection for the baldheaded bushy-browed teacher.

Jim was shocked to find several other professors had turned their backs on the infallibility of the Word of God. One professor in particular, Dr. Gear, never failed to let his students know they were wasting their time searching the Scriptures for truth.

In Jim's first year he stumbled on a book, *Jesus Came Preaching*. It described the power of preaching and the great things preachers had accomplished through the centuries. The book said, 'Jesus not only came preaching, but urged us to "Go and preach the Gospel."'

Jim also studied the great turn-of-the-century evangelist, Alexander White. When White saw the glory of preaching he said, 'If God has called you to be a preacher, don't stoop to be a king.' These words uprooted seeds of doubt the sepulchral doctor in Tampa had sown in Jim's heart. He was convinced preaching the gospel was the greatest calling in all the world.

He accepted every offer that came his way to speak in churches around the Southeast. One weekend he literally drove the wheels off Anne's car. On his way to speak at a church in South Carolina, the steering wheel jerked to the right, almost ripping itself out of his hands. The car lurched, bucked and began bouncing in a high-speed wobble. He maneuvered it to the shoulder and jumped out to inspect the damage.

Every tire was worn practically to the threads, but the right front had exploded. Its ghost ebbed away in a purplish blue haze as it expired. Jim kicked it.

He checked his watch, then ran to the back of the car. 'Please let there be a jack and tire irons,' he prayed as he opened the trunk. 'Yes! Thank you, Lord,' he said, looking toward heaven.

He stripped off his jacket, rolled up his shirtsleeves and got to work. It didn't take long to wrestle off the dead tire and replace it with the spare. He threw the tools along with the old tire into the trunk and slammed the lid. As he hurried to the driver's seat, he ran his hand along the side of the car. 'Lord, protect this vehicle. Get me safely to church and safely home. You know we can't afford new tires. We need you to provide.'

When he returned to the little garage apartment late that night, he wrapped his arms around Anne and kissed the top of her head. 'Oh, I missed you. But I'm glad you didn't go with me.'

'What?' Anne asked, pushing away from him. 'Why?'

Jim recounted the story of the blowout on the highway. 'It scared me to death. I thought I might have a head-on collision.'

'Jim! Are you all right?'

'Yes, and it was all worth it too.'

'Worth it? What could be worth ruining the car?'

'There was a high school choir visiting the church,' Jim said with a gleam in his eyes. 'I think the Lord divinely brought them today to hear the Gospel.' Jim grabbed Anne by the shoulders and asked, 'Guess what happened when I gave the invitation to receive Christ?'

'What?' Anne asked wide-eyed.

'Every one of those kids filed out of the choir loft behind me and knelt on the platform.'

'All of them?'

'Every single one. I was so blessed. I couldn't stop praising God all the way home. I wondered if Satan was trying to thwart me from going when I had the blowout. Now do you see what I mean when I said it was worth losing the tire?'

'Yes,' Anne said and hugged him tight. 'I'm so glad those kids got to hear the plan of salvation. I'm sure there was much rejoicing in heaven today when those precious children were won for Christ. But,' she said sobering.

'But what?'

'What are we going to do about the tires? That's our only transportation and I need it to get to work.'

'We can't forget that "God will supply all our needs according to His riches in glory." Where He guides, He always provides.' Jim closed his eyes and pulled Anne close. 'Lord,' he prayed. 'We thank you so much for the salvation of those children today. Thank you, too, that You have always provided everything we need. We know there is nothing too difficult for You, Lord. So we ask You for help. We need a new tire for our car. If we get another flat we'll be stuck. Thank You for hearing us, Lord. We trust You completely. In Jesus' name, Amen.'

'Amen,' Anne agreed.

As Jim went to class at Columbia the next day he saw a posse of clergy and elders from the South Carolina church where he had preached the day before. When they caught his eye they glared at him with stern frowns. Jim's stomach somersaulted and he wondered why they had driven all the way to the seminary.

After his class Dr. Gear cornered him. 'Now you've done it, Mr. Kennedy. I've heard how you ram Jesus down everyone's throat. You think everyone must have some kind of miraculous conversion as you did.' The professor shook his finger in Jim's face as if scolding a juvenile delinquent. 'Now you've gone too far. This is going to cost you one day.' The professor glared and stood for a moment seeming to wait for Jim to cower or cry.

Jim took a deep breath and straightened his shoulders. 'I don't think everyone must have an experience like mine. William, the pianist, doesn't remember when he accepted Christ. He grew up believing. I respect him and understand everyone's experience may come in a variety of ways. However, I do believe there is only one way to come to God and that is through his Son Jesus Christ. Acts 4:12 states, "Salvation is found in no one else, for there is no other name under heaven by which men must be saved." I will preach that with my dying breath.'

Dr. Gear's eye twitched and the corners of his mouth turned down in disapproval. 'That's according to your narrow interpretation, Mr. Kennedy,' he said with a humph, then turned abruptly and stalked away.

That afternoon Jim checked the mailbox before coming up the rickety staircase of their apartment. He shuffled quickly through the junk mail before stopping at a hand-addressed envelope with a Tampa return address. He flipped it over and pried up the flap.

He glanced quickly at the signature at the bottom and saw it was from a deacon in his old church, Bethel Presbyterian, in Clearwater. He scanned the letter as he climbed the steps, then stopped and reread it more carefully. 'Ha!' he laughed. 'I can't believe it. Anne!' he yelled and sprinted toward the door.

'Jim!' Anne called from the kitchen. 'What's wrong? Are you okay?'

'Anne, you'll never believe it,' he said breathing hard with excitement and exertion.

She turned around, holding the wooden spoon she had been using to stir their dinner. 'Dr. Gear accepted Jesus as his Savior?' she guessed.

'I wish!' Jim laughed. 'It's not that exciting. But it's still amazing. God is amazing!' he shouted at the ceiling.

Anne laughed. 'You are crazy, Jim! What happened?'

'Read it,' Jim said shaking the letter at her. 'Read it!'

Anne took the page and read,

Dear Jim and Anne,
You've been in Atlanta awhile now. Jim, I'm so proud that you are pursuing your divinity degree. I figured those old tires on Anne's car might be wearing thin from all your driving. You know I run the General Tire store here in Tampa. I've wired the store in Atlanta and let them know that you will be coming in to pick up four new tires. Hope all is well with you both. I'm looking forward to hearing Jim when he gets back.
God bless,
Mr. Lancaster

In the summers Jim and Anne moved back to Tampa so Jim could finish his bachelor's degree in English. When they came back to Atlanta for the next year of seminary Jim realized he needed to preach less on the weekends and study more. He threw himself into Old Testament, Hebrew, New Testament, Greek, systematic theology, hermeneutics and all the other -ologies and -ics the school had to offer.

That winter was one of the coldest on record. When the weatherman predicted sub-zero temperatures their landlord advised Jim to leave the water dripping in the tub to prevent the pipes from freezing.

The next morning he and Anne huddled together under a mound of blankets while their breath blew white vapors into the frigid room. Jim quoted, 'LORD, let me know my end, and what is the measure of my days; let me know how fleeting my life is! Behold, Thou hast made my days a few handbreadths, and my lifetime is as nothing in thy sight. Surely every man stands as a mere breath!' He punctuated the last word by exhaling a cloud of mist that hung in the air momentarily before dissolving.

'Ew, morning breath,' Anne said waving a hand in front of her face. 'Go brush your teeth before you kiss me. And turn up the heat!'

Jim rolled out of bed. 'Brr, it's freezing out here,' he said, jumping up and down in an effort to get warm. He checked the thermometer nailed above the window sill outside their bedroom. 'Ten above zero. The weatherman got close. But close only counts in horseshoes and hand grenades. If he were an Old Testament prophet we'd have to stone him.'

He shuffled into the bathroom. 'Good gracious!' he cried. 'Anne, you've got to see this.'

'I'm not getting out of this bed till the heat kicks on.' Her voice sounded muffled as she called from under the covers.

'You won't believe it.'

'What?' Anne peeped out.

'There's a stalagmite in our bath tub.'

'A what?'

'I guess it would be more proper to call it a stalactite.'

'Jim, I've told you not to speak in Greek. If you've got something to say, please say it in English.'

'It is English. You know, a stalactite grows down from the ceiling of a cave. It holds tight. Hence the name stalac-tite,' he said, emphasizing the end of the word.

Anne pulled the covers back over her head and gave a sigh of exasperation.

'I left the water running in the tub and it's frozen solid.' He jiggled the handle of the toilet. 'I hope you don't have to go. The potty is completely dysfunctional.'

'Oh, no!' Anne sat up suddenly. 'You're kidding?'

'I wish I were.'

Anne blew a lock of hair out of her eyes. 'Well this apartment does have one thing going for it.'

'What's that?' Jim asked as he twisted the hot water knob to see if anything would happen.

'The price!' Anne called then fell back, pulling the covers over her head.

16

WAIT AND SEE

'Your broadcast changed my life,' Jim told Donald Grey Barnhouse. The illustrious preacher had come to Atlanta to conduct a series of meetings. 'Sir, you are responsible for my salvation.' Barnhouse clapped him on the back. 'Tell me about it, son.'

As Jim recounted his conversion experience the older man's face mirrored surprise and delight. 'You'll have to come share that testimony at church one day soon,' Barnhouse said, gripping Jim's hand in a warm embrace.

During his time in seminary Jim had the opportunity to hear many great men teach. In his senior year, he was impressed by a preacher who called for laborers to enlist in foreign mission service. 'God commands everyone to go,' the preacher said. 'If you don't go you ought to have a good reason why not.'

Jim thought and prayed for days before deciding he didn't have a good reason to stay. Without consulting Anne he formally applied to the World Mission Committee as a candidate for missionary duty in the Belgian Congo (today, Zaire).

Later he shared his heart with Anne. 'I believe that God may want me to go to Africa. How do you feel about that?'

Anne stared at him with wide eyes. 'Where?' she asked.

'The Belgian Congo.'

'Oh, really?' she said slowly. 'Why there?'

'It's one of the toughest fields.'

'And you love a challenge.'

'Oh, Anne. You don't mind?' Jim asked sweeping her up in a warm embrace.

'Jim,' she said, pressing her cheek against his. 'I trust you're listening to God. How could I say no to Him. I know He'll direct you to wherever He wants. And where you go, I go.'

Jim busied himself studying the African interior. Atlases and books about the Congo littered their apartment. The most interesting lay open in stacks on their kitchen table so Anne could benefit from reading them too.

In the final weeks before graduation one of Jim's professors advised him to send out letters to the five presbyteries in Florida inquiring about pulpits that might still be unfilled.

'But I've applied for the Congo,' Jim responded.

'Yes, but you never know, the mission board could turn you down,' his professor said.

'Turned down? You must be joking. They need people desperately.'

'Just apply. You never know. You can do it with the stipulation that when you get the call from the World Mission Committee you'll have to leave. It may take awhile for them to process you and Anne. What else will you do in the meantime?'

Jim considered the counsel and sent out letters. This close to commencement, the most desirable posts were already taken. The only response came from Fort Lauderdale, Florida, on May 11, 1959 – only days before graduation.

The Home Mission Committee of the Everglades Presbytery was making an effort to organize a new church in the newly developing northern section of town. The small group of members had been taking turns meeting with whatever volunteers they could lure through advertisements and word of mouth. Jim came recommended by the pastor of Westminster Presbyterian Church and the president of the seminary. Both men represented the extremes in which the seminary had diverged since Columbia had taken a pronounced shift toward liberalism. Such a double recommendation was unusual and the committee was very interested in hearing from Rev. D. James Kennedy.

Jim became D. James Kennedy at his grandmother's bidding. After she prayed to receive Christ with him, she made a deathbed request for him to use his grandfather's name as a sobriquet.

When Jim arrived in Fort Lauderdale there wasn't a lot to encourage him in the way of a building, budget, organization or even congregation. He liked the name though. Coral Ridge Presbyterian Church had a nice ring to it. A large billboard stood in a sandy plot off sleepy 50th Street. The sign declared in large bold letters: 'Presbyterian Church To Be Built On This Site.'

Jim shaded his eyes with a hand and scanned the barren terrain in all directions. He walked along kicking the tall weeds and counting the nearby houses on one hand. It only lacked tumbleweeds to complete it as a desolate location. 'Well,' he said turning to face the anxious little group, 'it's a good place to have a church for field mice.'

They laughed and slapped his shoulder. 'Ha, a church for field mice,' they quoted. 'That's a good one.'

'Seriously,' Jim asked. 'Where will we meet?'

They drove him to a small elementary school located outside Fort Lauderdale, north in Pompano Beach. Jim strolled through the lunchroom which doubled as an auditorium. 'Its called a cafetorium,' one of the men explained.

'Cafetorium, that's a new one on me. Half cafeteria half auditorium, huh,' Jim said.

'I'm not sure if you'll find it in the dictionary, but that's what they call it here at McNab school,' the man said, and demonstrated how the lunch tables transformed into benches. Jim sat down on one to test it. 'I guess I won't have to worry about anyone falling asleep,' he quipped.

'Not too comfortable,' the men agreed.

Before Jim left to fly back to Atlanta he shook hands with the members of the committee. He agreed to temporarily fill the slot at Coral Ridge until he got the word from the World Mission Committee on when he'd leave for the Congo.

Jim had excelled academically in his three years at Columbia. He finished with cum laude distinction and won a graduate scholarship to Chicago's Graduate School of Theology. But his joy was short-lived. Soon after receiving this prize, he received a jolt that shook him to the core. He was informed, unceremoniously, that the faculty had voted to strip him of the scholarship because of his radical views on salvation.

Upon receiving this blow Jim went directly to his friend and mentor Dr. Gutzke. He paced back and forth as he recounted the dilemma to his professor. Dr. Gutzke stood, outwardly calm, as he listened intently. But his bushy brows belied his agitation. They bristled toward Jim like antenna receiving the waves of his frustration. The doctor's face darkened and he folded his enormous hands over his stomach. He spoke in a firm and authoritative voice. 'Jim,' he said, 'stand still and see the salvation of God.'

'But Dr. –'

The professor held up a hand to cut him off. 'Stand still and see the salvation of God.'

Jim nodded and took a deep breath. He reminded himself that God had always taken care of him. Like a jingle, he recited the truth again and again. 'Where God guides, God provides.'

As he walked through the school's hall, he encountered J. McDowell Richards, president of the seminary since 1932. He

was an even-tempered man who Jim had seen visibly upset on
only one occasion – when a prankster had hidden an alarm
clock in the chapel. Evidently it was set to ring at the precise
moment the guest speaker would be in the middle of his address
to the seminarians. When the man's voice crescendoed in his
discourse, a loud clang-alang-a-lang-a-lang interrupted him. At
first a few of the students snickered behind their hands, but
when Dr. Richards had jumped up, his face purple with rage,
all joviality had evaporated.

'Dr. Richards,' Jim said, as the elder man congratulated him
on his cum laude honor, 'may I have a word with you?'

'I just want to let you know that I do not think people must
come to Christ in the same way I did. I am not as rigid on this
point as I have been accused.'

Deep lines creased Dr. Richard's forehead. 'Who is accusing
you of what?' he asked with genuine surprise.

'Were you aware I was awarded one of the four graduate
scholarships?'

The president's face brightened. 'Well done, Jim.'

Jim shook his head. 'I was stripped of my award, sir.'

'You what?' Dr. Richard's voice registered disbelief.

'They say my doctrine of salvation is too radical. I have been
accused of forcing my views down people's throats. That is
completely false, sir. The only thing I am dogmatic about is that
Jesus Christ is the only way to God. I realize some may have
a dramatic conversion experience as Paul did on the road to
Damascus. But others may come as Timothy – through gradual
influence.'

Jim took a deep breath to calm his rapid pulse. 'I really
want the scholarship, Dr. Richards. Not only do I want to earn
a master's degree but also a doctorate. My desire is to study
to show myself approved unto God. No one should reject the
message of Christ because they believe I am not well educated,'
Jim said, remembering the comment by the outraged elder at
his church in Clearwater.

At each sentence Jim uttered the president of the seminary seemed to swell. His eye's bulged and the blue veins in his neck crept like long night crawlers beneath his skin.

Jim's face grew hot under the scrutiny of this illustrious man. He had not seen him so angry since the alarm clock incident. As several Columbia professors ambled down the hallway toward a graduate's reception, Dr. Richards waylaid them. He didn't say a word, but with a set jaw he jabbed his thick index finger at each man's chest, then jerked his thumb at his office. One by one every member of the faculty gathered in his study, then the president slammed the door.

Later, Dr. Gutzke reported to Jim what went on in that secret meeting. 'Dr. Richards deflated the inflated egos of the self-important instructors. When Dr. Gear made an effort to interrupt and defame you, the president cut him off with a curt hand gesture.' He demonstrated with a karate chop. '"We've heard enough from you already," Richards said through clenched teeth. "You reinstate Jim Kennedy's scholarship immediately. Immediately!" he bellowed.' Dr. Gutzke laughed. 'What did I tell you! What did I tell you?'

Jim reiterated Dr. Gutzke's prophesy, '"Stand still and see the salvation of God." You were right.' Jim bowed his head and thanked God. 'Lord,' he prayed, 'let me never worry again about anything. You said, "Be anxious for nothing. But in everything pray with thanksgiving and the peace of God will rule my heart and mind in Christ Jesus." I'll never forget.'

17

Scottish Revival

'Home sweet home,' Jim said as they pulled up to the motel in Fort Lauderdale. 'You can almost see the beach if you stand on the roof of the car.'

'Welcome to my little piece of paradise,' a voice boomed from the door of the motel office.

'Mr. Hedges!' Jim called. 'Thank you so much for giving us a reduced rate while we stay at your hotel.'

'No problem. I'm just glad you agreed to watch over her while I'm gone for the summer. Hello, Anne. It's so good to finally meet you,' Mr. Hedges said, extending his hand.

Anne took it and echoed Jim's thanks. 'We do appreciate this so much.'

The jovial motel owner cleared his throat. 'Well, let me show you around.' He waved for them to follow him into his office. 'Here's the Burlington Hotel office. But this is where you'll be spending most of your time, Anne.' He opened a door in the back of the office. Large washers and dryers hummed in cadence as they churned heavy loads of sheets and towels. 'Here's all the cleaning equipment.' He gestured toward the shelves which were lined with cleansers, rags, and scrub brushes. 'You'll have to change the sheets and towels every morning and mop the bathroom floor, clean the toilets, the sinks, the tub.' As Mr. Hedges ticked off the cleaning duties on his fingers Anne seemed to wilt more and more. She stretched her lips back in an effort to smile, but Jim saw the color drain from her face. He put his hand on her back to steady her and prevent her from turning and bolting out the door.

'When people call for reservations, write them down in this book. Here is the phone and here is where I keep the room keys.' He pointed at a wall filled with keys hanging on hooks. Numbers were written with black marker above each. Mr. Hedges pulled one of the keys off and handed it to Jim. 'You two make yourselves at home.'

'He's getting a pretty good deal out of us,' Anne said glancing over her shoulder at Mr. Hedges who waved and grinned. 'We'll be paying him to let me work as maid and caretaker.'

'It won't be for long. Think of it as training for the Congo. Really, compared to Africa, this ought to be easy.'

This news didn't seem to cheer Anne. She sighed heavily and wiped her forehead with a limp hand.

'I'll help as much as I can when I'm not busy with the new church,' Jim said wrapping an arm around her waist pulling her close. 'Let's just take it one day at a time.'

It didn't take them long to unpack. All their worldly belongings didn't add up to much. They stored their dishes and furniture in one room and settled into another. 'Hey,' Jim said rubbing his hands together, 'Let's go to church.'

Jim drove Anne to the McNab Elementary School. The sun sank low and shadows slanted in long arms across the parking lot. Jim fished a key to the cafetorium from his pocket and opened the door.

'Wow,' Anne said as she walked the length of the room. 'So this is where it all begins.'

'At least till we hear from the World Missions Organization,' Jim said as he tilted one of the tables to convert it into a bench.

'Clever,' Anne said admiring the prospective pew. 'It actually looks remarkably like –,' she paused inspecting it, 'overturned cafeteria tables.'

Jim laughed. 'Your description is, as always, astute, my love.' He walked toward the wall of windows. 'It's a little stuffy. But the air conditioning in this building is heaven-sent,' he said and cranked the glass open.

Anne closed her eyes and inhaled deeply. 'Nice. Thank you Lord for the ocean breeze.'

Jim wrapped his arms around her and kissed her forehead. 'You are such a good sport. I'm so thankful to the Lord for you. I'm excited and nervous all at the same time. This little room will be my first church. I have a responsibility to everyone who comes.'

Anne squeezed Jim. 'I know God will use you in a mighty way.'

'I hope so, Anne. I pray so.'

The next week Jim was busy. He put an advertisement in the local paper inviting people to come to the new Coral Ridge Presbyterian Church: 'Services will begin in the McNab Elementary Cafetorium at 8:30 a.m. Sunday morning.' Jim winced at the early hour, but another up-and-coming church had the 11:00 a.m. slot.

Jim spent much of his time preparing his sermon. He pored over the old sermons of Spurgeon, Luther and Calvin.

Many residents of the motel wondered at the sonorous voices that boomed from the Kennedy's room. They spoke short sentences then were cut off as if someone turned a switch. A different person repeated the words then the authoritative voice continued – stop – second man repeated the words – stop – first voice started again – stop –.

Anne walked into the room, huffed out a deep breath and collapsed onto the bed. She lifted red hands and frowned. 'Look at my hands,' she moaned.

Jim reached over and grabbed one of her raw palms. 'You poor thing,' he said and kissed her fingers. 'You've been working too hard. How can I help?'

Anne fanned the air. 'I'm fine. I just wanted a little sympathy.' She motioned toward the window. 'You should see the looks this room is getting from folks out there. Maybe you should turn down that record player. They must think you're holding Charlton Heston hostage in here.'

'Listen to his voice.' Jim put the needle onto the record, closed his eyes and balled his fingers into a fist. 'He has such a marvelous command of speech. If I listen to him and other great orators and practice their voice inflections, I think it would make a big difference in the pulpit.'

'I can't wait till Sunday. You've been working so hard, I know your sermon will be life-changing.'

'God willing.' Jim nodded. 'I want to be a tool in His hand to make a difference in this city. Until we head to Africa that is.'

'Yes, Africa.' Anne nodded and glared at her hands. 'Can't wait,' she said flatly.

Jim could hardly sleep Saturday night. He kept waking up, afraid he had overslept and missed his first day to preach. He'd lean over, grab the alarm clock and squint at the luminous dial. '3:00 a.m.,' he'd groan and flop back onto his pillow. Finally, at 5:00, he got up.

'I'm going to throw you back in the ocean, you fish-out-of-water. You tossed and turned all night,' Anne said throwing her pillow at him.

'I couldn't sleep,' he confessed.

'Really?' she said in a sarcastic tone. 'I couldn't either for some reason.' She reached out and laid her hand on his arm, 'I'm sorry. I know this is your big day. Are you ready?'

'Yes, I'm just a little nervous. I'm going to pray.'

'Love you,' Anne said and rolled over for an hour of peaceful sleep.

They arrived at the cafetorium at 7:45. Jim sniffed, then wrinkled his nose. 'Sour milk.'

Anne began opening windows. 'Think of the hundreds of kids who eat in here every day of the week. I'm sure dozens spill their milk on the tables and floor. The breeze will freshen it up a bit.'

'Breeze?' Jim said. 'What breeze?'

'It will come – eventually.'

The tables had been clicked down into benches and Anne organized some child-sized wooden chairs into rows. 'Look someone carved our initials on this one. It says, "A.L. + J.K.".'

'Well, this one says, "A.L. + P.W." I want to know who P.W. is, Anne Lewis.'

'Those aren't my initials anyway,' Anne said as she inspected the carvings on the other chairs. 'I'll have to carve, A.K. + J.K. now.'

'Better not. I'm sure the school would frown on the minister's wife whittling on their chairs.'

'Who could tell?' she asked. 'There's so much scratched on them now, I don't think one more would make a difference.'

Jim pointed to an old upright in the corner. 'Look, A.K., why don't you play some hymns and pray someone shows up.'

Anne sat on the bench and played the C scale from one end of the keyboard to the other. She winced twice. 'Needs a little tuning, but it's a start.' She began to play.

'That sounds wonderful. Here come some people now,' he whispered excitedly. 'Keep playing.'

Jim walked to the back and began greeting the newcomers. A member of the committee who had hired him brought in a stack of mimeographed bulletins. On the front they read,

June 21, 1959

Coral Ridge Presbyterian Church

We are happy to have Mr. James Kennedy, who, by appointment of the Presbytery of the Everglade, has come to be our

Pastor and to lead us toward an organized Presbyterian Church in our community.

At 8:30 sharp Reverend D. James Kennedy opened the service with a welcome to the 45 people who showed up for his first service. He gestured toward Anne, 'My lovely wife, Anne, will grace us with a solo to prepare our hearts for worship.'

She gave a little wave over the top of the piano before she began to play and sing a familiar hymn. As the sound of her voice filled the room, Jim closed his eyes and silently asked the Lord to speak through him as he led this new church. When Anne finished, she took her seat in one of the child-sized chairs. Jim thanked her and she flashed him a wide smile. He took a deep breath and plunged into his first message.

Jim preached a sound doctrinal sermon full of his love and zeal for Jesus Christ. He purposefully stared into the eyes of each person in the congregation searching for any spark of enlightenment. At the end of his sermon he closed his eyes, gripped the top corners of the lectern and said, 'If you've never invited Jesus into your heart, you can do so right now with me.' He paused a moment to let this statement sink in, then continued. 'Now, as every head is bowed and *every eye closed*, slip up your right hand if you want to invite Jesus to be your Savior and Lord.'

When Jim looked up to count the saved souls, he received a jolt of surprise. He couldn't believe it. He had expected maybe one or two hands to be raised, but not this.

No one had bowed. No eyes were closed. A crowd of critical faces stared disconcertingly back at him. Jim swallowed hard, closed his eyes and repeated with emphasis, 'Every head bowed, and every eye closed.' He peeked up to see if any followed his cue.

One woman on the front row folded her arms across her chest and glared. He closed his eyes again and quickly finished his prayer. Anne had slipped behind the piano and started playing the doxology at his 'Amen.' He walked quickly to the back of the room as the music praised God from whom all blessings flow. Taking his position by the door, he prepared to greet each person as they left.

The silver-haired woman who had glared at him from the front row click, click-clicked quickly across the floor in her high-heeled shoes. As she approached, Jim stuck his hand out in a friendly gesture. 'Thank you for –.'

'What kind of cult is this?' she said cutting him off. In spite of the warmth of the day, she drew the lapels of her mink stole around her neck as if it would protect her from some infectious disease Jim might foist upon her. She sniffed loudly, raised her chin and turned her head in one swift motion before exiting haughtily.

A small man in a rumpled coat that smelled of moth balls came next. 'Thank you, pastor,' he said with a thick Brooklyn accent.

'You must not be from around here.' Jim smiled in an effort to cover the blow the silver-haired woman dealt him.

'You're pretty sharp,' the man said and winked. 'I guess my sunburn gives me away.'

'Right,' Jim said slowly.

When everyone filed out, Jim looked at Anne. 'How do you think it went?'

'Great. I didn't expect so many people our first Sunday.'

'I don't think anyone is actually from Florida.'

'What about the lady who brought the gladioli?' Anne gestured to the front of the room where a bunch of bright red flowers stood doing their best to look cheerful.

Jim surveyed the room. 'I wonder how long before we outgrow this cafetorium?'

'Ten is a good round number,' Anne said. 'I'd say in ten months we'll be bulging at the seams. That is, if we aren't in the Congo by then. But at least we can have this church up and running for someone else to take over.'

'One lady asked if this was some kind of cult,' Jim said with a chuckle.

'You're kidding?'

Jim frowned and shook his head.

'Remember the farmer and the mosquitoes? Do with insults what the farmer does with mosquitoes?'

'Swat them?'

'No, silly. Ignore them.'

Three months later, as Anne performed her maid duties, the postman arrived with a handful of letters for the motel residents. She walked into the office, picked up the stack of mail, and began to sort it. A long white envelope addressed to D. James Kennedy caught her attention. She lifted it with trembling fingers as she read the return address: World Mission Committee.

'Jim!' she yelled and took off running toward their room. She burst through the door waving the letter. 'It's here! The mission board has finally written to tell us when we're going!'

He was buried behind his Bible and commentaries preparing for Sunday's sermon. He jumped up, scattering the books. 'Have you read it?' he asked.

Anne gasped to catch her breath. Her eyes danced as she shook her head. 'I wanted you to see it first.'

Jim took the envelope and ran his finger around the lip in one motion. He tore out the page inside and unfolded it. 'Dear Mr. Kennedy,' he read aloud, quickly scanning the first lines. 'Thank you for applying, blah, blah, blah, when do I go?' he said, running his finger down the sentences. 'Here! It says –,' his lips mouthed the words as he silently read their destiny, then he looked up at Anne with wide eyes.

'What? When?' she said with a laugh then sobered. 'Jim, what's the matter?'

'You read it,' he said, opening his hand and letting the letter fall from his fingers.

Anne snatched it up and scanned it briefly, mumbling the lines unintelligibly. 'They aren't accepting us,' she said flatly.

'No,' he corrected, 'they aren't accepting me. My asthma has disqualified me once again.'

'Oh, Jim,' Anne said wrapping her arms around his neck and kissing his cheek. 'I love you. I know you really wanted to go to the mission field.'

'Ask me anything about the Congo,' Jim said. 'I've studied so much about it, and I've had my heart set on going.'

'It's okay,' Anne said soothingly. 'Now you can focus all your attention on building this church.'

Jim sighed heavily. 'You're just saying that because it's failing.'

'It's not failing. It's true some people have left, but more will come. Maybe you should go see the visitors. We have their addresses on the pew cards.'

'You're right. I will. Now that I know I'm going to be here for the long haul my attention won't be divided between Africa and Fort Lauderdale.'

'And we can worship at the 11:00 a.m. hour at McNab school now,' Anne said.

'Yes, but you kind of hate to be glad about that other church folding.'

'I guess if their pastor hadn't slept in he'd still be preaching the 11:00 hour. Nobody's going to come to church if the pastor fails to show up.'

'Too bad he didn't have a good wife like I do to make sure he was up and going.'

'You're the one up praying at the crack of dawn,' Anne said and laughed. She was quiet a moment and pensive. When she looked up, Jim saw lines of concern on her forehead. 'Jim,' she asked. 'Now that we know we aren't going to the Congo, can we look around for a permanent place to live? I'm tired of cleaning other people's toilets and making their beds. The only bathrooms I want to clean are my own. Dad said he'd help us with a down payment on a house.'

Jim laughed. 'I thought you were going to tell me something awful by the look on your face. Yes! Definitely. Let's go right now. I'll grab a couple of address cards, and we can stop by some of the church visitors' homes on our way.'

Six months later Jim stood in the pulpit and counted heads as Anne and two other women from their foundling church sang a trio. 'Lord,' he prayed silently. 'I don't understand. What am I doing wrong? Have I misunderstood your calling?'

As the women harmonized, 'Amen,' Jim stood and forced a smile. 'Good morning everyone. Turn in your Bible's to –.'

After the service, as he locked the doors to the McNab Cafetorium, Anne laid her hand on his back. His shoulders slumped at her touch and he turned toward her. 'Oh, Anne. I'm sorry I've brought you here and made you suffer.'

'Suffer? Jim, what ever are you talking about?'

'Seventeen.'

'Seventeen?' Anne repeated.

Jim sighed heavily. 'Yes, seventeen. Didn't you count. Don't you remember what you said our first Sunday here?'

Anne looked up at the sky and tapped her chin as if trying to remember.

Jim grabbed her hand and said, 'Don't be silly. I'm serious. You said it would only take about ten months for us to be bursting at the seams. It's almost ten months now and we're experiencing a Scottish Revival.'

'Scottish Revival?'

'Yes, we've gone from 45 to 17.'

'I noticed you didn't give an invitation at the end of the service today. Why not?' Anne asked.

'One of the elders told me it might be one of the reasons people aren't coming back. Most folks down here aren't used to the southern style altar call. Most are snowbirds who fly down from New York, Illinois and Ohio for the winter or to retire.

He said they think it's offensive. I need to find another way to reach them besides an altar call.'

'Maybe if you tried visiting more people.'

'You remember what happened last time I did that.'

'Oh, yeah,' Anne said, pinching the bridge of her nose between her thumb and third finger. 'That was something!'

'I don't want anything to do with your sawdust religion!' Jim mimicked the high voice of the woman he had visited earlier. He rubbed his nose. 'My nose still smarts where she slammed the door on it.'

'Very funny,' Anne said. 'Oh, Honey. You are the Arthur Murray salesman of the year. You wouldn't let that get you down if you were selling dancing lessons.'

'But this is the gospel. I'm not selling it. It's the free gift of God for eternal life.' Jim stood for a moment brooding silently. He turned to Anne, his countenance brightening. 'You're right. I need to go back out and visit people. But Jesus sent his disciples out in pairs. I'll ask one of my elders to go with me. It will be killing two birds with one stone. I'll get to lead someone to Christ and train someone to share their faith at the same time.'

18

Sic 'em

'Who are we going to see?' the elder asked Jim as they drove together on their first church visitation.

Jim held the information card between his index and middle finger. The shaky handwriting suggested a little old lady was the author. Jim remembered a sweet gray-haired woman tottering over to shake his hand after his sermon. He thought she should be an easy first candidate for him to demonstrate to his elder how to share the gospel. He smiled as he recited her name. 'Mrs. Jones. Do you recall meeting her?'

The elder shook his head. 'Nope, but I'm about to. This is the address right here.'

'Let's pray before we go in,' Jim said.

The two men bowed their heads. 'Lord, thank You for your salvation that You have given us so freely. I pray that Mrs. Jones will be open to hearing Your gospel. Please, lead us by Your Holy Spirit and direct our words as we share with her. In Jesus' name, Amen.'

'Amen,' the elder agreed.

Jim lifted the knocker with confidence and rap, rapped it against the door. He turned and smiled at his friend. The man put his hands together and looked heavenward, pantomiming a prayer. Jim nodded thanks, then straightened his tie and cleared his throat as they waited on the stoop.

Thud, thud, thud. Jim raised his brows in surprise when he heard heavy footfalls coming from behind the door. He quickly checked the address on the card and glanced up to the door to make sure they were at the right house. The door flung wide and Jim fumbled the card then caught it again as he stared up at the large person who opened the door.

'What do you want?' a gruff voice asked behind a bushy-bearded face.

'We-we, is-is this,' Jim glanced down at the card again. 'Is this 1992 Moss Street?'

'Yes.'

'Does Mrs. Jones live here?'

'My mom. Yeah, she lives here.'

'Is she at home?'

'No.'

'Oh, too bad,' Jim said. His tone betrayed his relief.

'What did you want with her?' the man asked, narrowing his eyes and talking around the glowing cigar clenched between his teeth. 'You sellin' somethin'?'

'Oh, no,' Jim raised his hands palms out. 'I'm the pastor of a church she has attended and we just stopped by for a visit.'

'Pastor, huh. Well come on in.' The man stepped sideways and waved them in with the beer can clutched in his right hand. A tattoo of a black snake baring its fangs wound its way across his bicep. Its angry red eyes seemed to follow Jim and the elder as they squeezed past.

'Uh, thanks,' Jim said, trying not to stare at the man's arm.

The elder gave Jim a thumbs-up sign. But Jim furrowed his brows and puckered his lips in a silent, 'Sh!'

'Have a seat, fellows.'

Jim swung around and grinned. 'Thanks,' he said, taking a quick survey of the furniture. Between forefinger and thumb, he gingerly picked up a black banana peel then set it along with a couple of beer cans on the floor before sitting on the sofa. The elder shoved the rest of the cans to the side and perched next to him.

'How 'bout a cold one?' Mrs. Jones' son asked as he popped the tab on a Miller can. A haze of tiny bubbles spit and sputtered from the opening.

'Uh, thanks. No. No thanks that is. Well,' Jim cleared his throat, 'how are you?'

'Great,' the man said keeping his eyes fixed on the baseball game that blared on a black and white television set.

'Weather's nice lately, huh? Not so hot,' Jim said glancing toward the window.

'Yeah,' the man said with a grunt.

'Who are you pulling for?' Jim pointed at the T.V.

The elder elbowed Jim sharply. 'Sic 'em,' he whispered out of the corner of his mouth.

Jim glared at him and hissed, 'Hush, man. Do you want to get us killed.'

'What was that?' the burly fellow said looking at them suspiciously.

Jim grabbed a beer can at his feet. 'Spilled,' he said with a nervous laugh. 'I didn't want it to be spilled,' he said with emphasis on the last word. 'Well, Mr. Jones, may I call you that?'

'Whatever,' the man said and belched.

'I think we'd better get going. It was nice visiting with you. Tell your mother we stopped by.' Jim stood and motioned behind his back for the elder to follow.

As they walked out the front door, Jim sighed heavily. His shoulders sagged and he glanced at the elder out of the corner of his eye then looked away quickly. 'I suddenly remembered

I had to do something important,' he mumbled as he opened the door of the car.

The drive back seemed to take longer than the drive there. The two men sat in silence as thick as the humidity of a south Florida summer. 'Bye,' Jim said weakly as he dropped the elder off at his home.

'I'm a failure,' Jim moaned as he drove along. He didn't want to go home and face Anne, so he drove to the coast and parked. He got out of his car and walked toward the water. The hush and swish of the waves seemed to mock. 'Fail -ure,' they said over and over in their relentless beating against the shore. Jim plopped down on the beach and lay back in the sand.

As he stared into the sky, he remembered lying on the shores of Lake Michigan as a kid. The old longing of his past arose in his soul. 'I know you're up there, God,' he said to the expanse. 'I know you've got to have more for me than this.' He threw a handful of sand over his shoulder. He lay still and cupped his ear. 'I'm listening,' he whispered. 'Why am I here? Tell me what you want. I know you must have a purpose for me.'

He half expected his brother, George, to kick sand in his face and tell him his purpose was to go deliver groceries. He felt a little silly lying in the sand fully clothed. He sat up, propped his elbows on his knees, and stared at the waves. The dark water stretched out as far as he could see till the earth met the stars on the horizon. He felt small and unimportant in God's grand scheme.

The next Sunday Jim preached to 17 people.

'We might as well stop calling it church, Anne,' he said after the service. 'Why not call it a Bible study. At this rate, in twelve months, everybody will have dropped out.'

After the service, Jim and Anne drove to their new home in silence. When they arrived, Jim opened the door for Anne. 'I'm so glad you don't have to work as a maid in that motel anymore,' he said. 'I just hope we'll be here long enough to enjoy this place,' he mumbled under his breath as he closed the door.

'What dear?' Anne asked turning toward him.

'Nothing,' Jim said as he loosened his tie.

The next day a letter arrived in the mail that would change everything. Unaware his world was about to be turned upside down, Jim glanced at the return address before ripping it open. Kennedy Smartt, pastor of Inggleside Presbyterian Church, Scottsdale, Georgia, was printed on the top left corner. Jim had attended Inggleside some when he was in seminary. He had even preached in the pulpit as a guest speaker.

He read the letter with a mixture of relief and reluctance then chuckled to himself. 'You've got quite a sense of humor, Lord.'

Anne walked into the room and saw him grinning over the page in his hand. 'What's so funny?'

Jim held the letter out. 'Read this.'

Anne took it. 'Oh,' she said, 'It's from Kennedy Smartt. I always enjoyed going to his church when we were in Atlanta.' She scanned the letter. 'This is great. It's just what you need. A week away from Fort Lauderdale will do you good.'

'But, Anne,' Jim said, 'he wants me to conduct ten days of evangelistic services.'

'I can read,' she said, waving the page at him.

Jim nodded. 'Yes, but I've just about decimated Coral Ridge Presbyterian. What if I bring the plague across states lines and wipe out Inggleside Presbyterian?'

'You're such a comedian,' Anne said and poked Jim in the chest. 'You are a great pastor and teacher. You are great at sharing the gospel. This is a gift from the Lord. Spending ten days with Kennedy Smartt and getting to preach in Atlanta will be very encouraging.'

'You're right. I thought so, too. Maybe people in Georgia will respond to the gospel better than the people in Florida. I'll give him a call and tell him I'll come.'

19

TOUGH NUTS

When Jim arrived in Atlanta, Kennedy Smartt greeted him at the airport. 'Hey, brother!' He threw an arm around Jim's shoulder and squeezed. 'I'm glad you could come. I remember what a marvelous evangelist you were in seminary. I've told my congregation how you led your fellow seminary student from Sweden to Christ.'

'Oh yeah, Henrich,' Jim said, closing his eyes and recalling the memory. 'We were walking between the red brick buildings under the big oak trees on campus.' He opened his eyes and stared into the distance as if reliving the moment. 'I couldn't believe he didn't understand anything about the real meaning of salvation. All I did was share my testimony.'

'I remember how annoyed everyone on campus was that you had the audacity to share Christ with a fellow seminary student,' Kennedy Smartt said. 'They thought you did him a great discourtesy.'

'I didn't do anything,' Jim laughed. 'Henrich made his decision to follow Christ then came to your church.'

'That's why I wanted you to come up for this conference,' Kennedy said slapping Jim on the back. 'I want my congregation to hear from a man with such a passion for sharing his faith.'

'Great,' Jim said, smiling as he remembered his recent evangelism fiasco.

'You'll be preaching every night.'

That's wonderful,' Jim said patting his briefcase filled with several sermons he had already prepared.

'However,' Kennedy said raising his brows significantly, 'that's not the most important thing.'

A cold chill of foreboding ran up Jim's back. He shuddered involuntarily. 'No, of course not?' Jim said mustering a confident facade.

'The most important thing, as you already know,' he said as they walked through the parking lot to his car, 'is we'll go out every morning, afternoon and sometimes at night after the services and share our faith door-to-door.'

'Door-to-door,' Jim said, forcing a smile over dry teeth. 'Great.' He reached up to loosen his tie and gulped.

Kennedy didn't seem to notice Jim's discomfort. 'And,' he continued, 'you're going to have an opportunity to witness to these people eyeball-to-eyeball and toenail-to-toenail. And,' he said, raising a hand and grinning widely, 'I have saved all the tough nuts for you to crack.'

Jim forced a hollow laugh. He thought, *thanks a lot, buddy*, but said aloud, 'That's great. You know, we professional evangelists don't fool with anything but tough nuts.'

As Kennedy Smartt walked to the driver's seat Jim mumbled under his breath, 'There's one problem, however; I came to Atlanta to tell you I wouldn't be able to come. There's a funeral you're going to have here in town if I don't get out quickly.'

'What's that Jim?' Kennedy asked, as he slammed his door.

'Nothing.' Jim cleared his throat and said again in a lower tone, 'Nothing. A frog in my throat.'

Kennedy drove Jim to a hotel and helped carry his bags to his room. 'Get a good night's sleep. I'll pick you up in the morning and we'll hit the streets.'

Jim nodded. 'Sure. Good night.'

He stumbled toward the bed and fell to his knees clasping his hands together like a young boy saying his prayers before sleeping. 'Lord,' he cried. 'Oh, Lord, what am I going to do? I don't know how to witness to anybody. Kennedy Smartt is going to watch 'Kennedy dumb' make a fool of himself.'

Jim winced at the thought. 'It's like asking a new medical student to perform a difficult surgery. It's impossible.'

'Lord, you've got to help me! Why did I agree to come up here?' He looked up at the ceiling, his face brightening. 'I've got it, Lord. If you'll return tonight it will solve all my problems. Oh, Lord. Please come back right now, right now.' He squeezed his eyes closed and begged, 'Tonight, Lord. Return tonight.'

He lay flat on the hotel bed exhaling in a noisy sigh. 'Do something. Lord, please, do something. Anything.' Jim continued praying for what seemed hours. The sun pierced the curtains and drove its beam between his closed lids. Jim threw a hand over his face and rolled over. 'Oh, Anne,' he mumbled. 'I had the worst dream.' He reached across the bed to embrace his wife. He tapped his hand up toward the pillow then down. 'Anne?' He sat up abruptly opening his eyes wide. 'Oh, no!' he moaned and flopped back onto the pillows. 'It wasn't a dream.'

Reluctantly, he dragged himself out of bed and wove a groggy path to the bathroom where he squinted into the mirror. He reached up and pulled his rumpled tie from his neck and unbuttoned his wrinkled shirt. 'I must have fallen asleep while I prayed,' he muttered to himself. 'I see you decided not to return last night, Lord,' he said glancing up. 'Thanks a lot.'

He splashed water on his face and brushed his teeth vigorously before shaving and getting dressed. Kennedy Smartt knocked a rapid tattoo on his door. Jim shaded his eyes as the sun streamed in behind his friend. 'Ready?' he asked.

Jim nodded and grabbed his Bible, tucking it into his briefcase.

At their first stop Kennedy talked rapidly as he explained how they got the addresses of people they would be visiting. Jim nodded uncomprehendingly. He couldn't concentrate on the pastor's monologue with his heart hammering in his ears.

At their first stop, Rev. Smartt hammered on the doorknocker and winked at Jim. 'Isn't this great!' he said and rubbed his hands together gleefully.

'Great,' Jim said trying to sound enthusiastic. He thought he might throw up.

It took a while for someone to come to the door. Jim had just turned to say, 'Too, bad. No one is here,' when the door swung open behind him. Discordant music beat uneven rhythms in the background reminiscent of tennis shoes tumbling in the dryer. Jim turned and faced the bellybutton of the man in the doorway. He looked up and swallowed hard. 'Your last name doesn't happen to be Jones?' he asked, wondering if Mrs. Jones' other son had moved to Georgia.

With a thick pink tongue, the man rolled his cigar to the other side of his mouth before answering. 'Jones,' he said in a husky voice. 'Never heard of 'em.'

Kennedy Smartt barged past the goliath. 'Good to see you, Hank,' he said. 'I've brought someone I want you to meet.' He turned back and beckoned for Jim to follow. 'This is Jim Kennedy. He's a professional evangelist. I've brought him here to talk to you about your soul.'

Jim gulped, looked up at the large man and waved. 'Hello.'

Hank led Jim and Kennedy into his living room which was remarkable in its decor because it so closely resembled his unknown twin's in Fort Lauderdale. Jim cleared his throat and began a speech that sounded remarkably close to a sales pitch for Arthur Murray, minus the down payment of cash. 'Hank, I can tell by just looking around your house, you need God.' Jim stared pointedly at the beer cans littering the floor.

Hank's face turned red and he made a sound in the back of his throat that closely resembled the growl of an angry rottweiler.

'I mean, there is no way *you* can ever please God. You've got to turn from your wicked ways. Repent!' Jim punctuated the word by jabbing a finger at Hank's chest.

The big man's face turned crimson and he erupted from his chair spewing ash from his cigar. 'Why you!'

Jim jumped backward. 'Now, Hank. It's true. We are all sinners in the hands of an angry God. God hates sin, but even the good things you do are filthy rags to God. Now, Hank, wait, I'm not finished,' he said and stepped behind the chair, wielding it as a shield.

Hank lunged to the right of the chair as Jim stepped left almost shouting, 'Ole!'

At this point Kennedy Smartt jumped between Hank and Jim placing his hand on the larger man's wide forearm. 'Hank, let me ask you a question.'

Hank turned blazing eyes toward Reverend Smartt. 'What?' he demanded, his hands clenched into white-knuckled fists.

'Hank, wait. Calm down. Just answer one question for me?'

The large man scowled. 'What is it?' he demanded.

'If you died tonight, how sure are you that you'd go to heaven?'

Hank froze. The fire in his eyes died and they clouded over. 'I've actually been worrying about that lately,' he said in a subdued tone.

'What if I could tell you how to know for sure that when you die you can go to heaven? Would you be interested?'

'Sure, who wouldn't,' the big man said, dropping back onto the couch.

'You know, Hank, this is why the Bible was written. It says, "These things are written ... that you may know you have eternal life."'

'Really?'

'Yes. Let me ask you another question.'

'Shoot.'

Smartt asked the question he had heard Jim use before. 'Suppose you were to die today and stand before God and He were to say to you, "Hank, why should I let you into my heaven?" What would you say?'

'I've tried to be good. I've gone to church.' He paused. 'Not all the time, but I've gone. You know me pastor. That's how you got my name. I came to your church.'

'Yes, Hank, I'm glad you came to Inggleside. Is there anything else you would say to God?'

'I'm better than a lot of other people I know,' he said pointing toward the door.

'I'm sure you are,' Kennedy Smartt nodded. 'You know, Hank, most of us think we've got to be good enough to get to heaven. We have to earn our way. Follow the rules. But the Bible tells us that heaven and eternal life are free. There's nothing we can do to earn them.'

'What do you mean?' Hank asked and hunched forward in his chair.

'The Bible says what we earn for our sins – lying, cursing, cheating or even hating someone – results in death or separation from God. But God's free gift is eternal life through Jesus Christ our Lord. It's a gift. You can't earn a gift can you? It's given freely out of love.'

Hank dug his knuckle into the corner of his eye, quickly dodging out a tear. 'Allergies,' he said with a sniff.

'I have allergies too,' Jim said in an effort to find common ground.

Hank glared at him momentarily then cleared his throat and asked, 'How do you get the gift?'

'We can't save ourselves,' Smartt continued. 'The Bible says if we keep every law but offend in one point we are guilty of all of them. It's like a bit of arsenic in your beverage. Just a drop will kill you. Since all have sinned and no one is perfect, we must pay the penalty – death. The Bible states clearly we aren't saved by the good things we have done, but God saved us according to his mercy. By grace – something we don't deserve, but God gives us anyway – we are saved through faith. Faith is putting our full trust in God and acting on what he says is true. It is not something we can earn. Otherwise we'd be boasting saying, "I'm better than that guy." If we could be good enough to get to God, how would we know if we'd been good enough?'

Hank nodded. 'So faith is just believing?'

'Saving faith is not just head knowledge, believing historical facts. The Bible says even the devil believes there is one God, so just believing in God is not enough to save us. It is trusting in Jesus Christ alone for eternal life. It means resting upon Christ alone and what he has done for us rather than in what you or I have done that will get us into Heaven.

'Hank, would you like to receive the gift of eternal life?'

'Yes, I do want to. How?'

'Let's clarify what it involves:

● It means you need to transfer your trust from what you have been doing to what Christ has done for you on the cross.

● It means to accept Christ as Savior. Open your heart and invite Him to come in, forgive your sins, and give you eternal life. Jesus says, "Behold, I stand at the door and knock: if any man hear My voice, and opens the door, I will come in to Him...."

● It means to receive Jesus Christ as Lord. Give Him the "driver's seat" and "controls" of your life, not the "back seat."

● It means to repent. Be willing to turn from anything not pleasing to Him. He will reveal His will to you as you grow in your relationship with Him.'

'Is this what you really want, Hank?'

Hank nodded. 'Yes,' he said, his voice cracking.

'You can go to God in prayer right now, here in this room. Prayer is just talking to God. If you want you can repeat after me.'

Hank nodded.

Kennedy began, 'Lord Jesus...'

'Lord Jesus,' Hank repeated.

'I know I am a sinner and don't deserve eternal life, but I believe You paid for all my sins when You died on the cross then rose from the grave.'

Hank repeated the words with a loud sniff.

'Come in and take control of my life, forgive my sins and save me. I repent of my sins and now place my trust in You for my salvation. I accept the free gift of eternal life. Amen.'

'Amen,' Hank said after he finished the prayer.

Kennedy Smartt reached out and grabbed Hank's hand. 'We're brothers now. You are in the family of God.'

Hank pumped his hand hard and laughed. 'Amazing,' he rasped.

'What do you think you should do now?' Kennedy asked.

'Go to church?' Hank asked.

'When a baby is first born it needs lots of milk. The milk for Christians is the Bible. It is important for you to spend time every day reading the Word of God. Do you have a Bible?'

'Yeah, I think. Hang on a second.'

Hank lumbered down the hall. His heavy footsteps shook the floor causing the empty beer cans to ching softly.

Jim stared wide-eyed at Kennedy. 'How'd you learn to do that?' he whispered in awe.

'Last year Bill Iverson was the speaker at our Evangelistic Outreach. I went out with him and this is what he did. He was a tough cookie. You know he played football at Davidson. One fellow we met said he was an atheist. Without a pause, Bill asked, 'How long have you been running around with another woman who is not your wife?"

'No!' Jim asked, his brow furrowing. 'He didn't.'

'Yes! And do you know what the man did?'

'What?'

'He burst into tears. He asked Bill how he knew.'

'Good night!' Jim exclaimed. 'Did he come to Christ?'

'Sure did.'

Hank came bounding back, brushing off the Bible he clutched in his hand. 'It's a little dusty,' he said with a crooked grin.

'It's great,' Kennedy assured him. He took the Bible and flipped through the stiff pages till he came to the book of John. 'Here's a great place to start. This book tells all about Jesus' life and ministry. Prayer is also important. Try to set aside time to talk to God. And talk to him all day – everywhere you go, any time, day or night. God never slumbers nor sleeps.

'And come to church. We'd love to have you.' He turned to John 4:24 and read, "God is a Spirit: and they that worship Him must worship Him in spirit and truth." 'Also, it is important to have fellowship. That is just a fancy word for hanging out with other believers. That way you can encourage each other. Several logs will burn brightly together, but if you take one away the fire goes out.'

Hank nodded. 'Yeah, I've seen that happen before.'

'When we are around other people who love God,' Kennedy said, 'it ignites our passion for him. Just like the flaming logs.' 'Also,' he continued, 'tell someone about your new life in Christ. That's called witnessing. Tell them what Christ has done in your life. Why don't you come to church tonight. We're having a rally. You could tell everyone how you trusted Christ today.'

'I will. I will, pastor. Thank you so much for helping me understand how I can know God.' He turned to Jim and his face darkened briefly, then cleared as if the sun had come out and melted the clouds. He grinned and stuck his hand out. 'You could learn a thing or two from this fellow,' he said jerking his chin toward Kennedy Smartt.

'You're right,' Jim said. 'We share the same name, you know. We're both Kennedys.'

'Really?' Hank asked.

'But you can know the difference between him and me because he's the smart one – Kennedy Smartt.'

The rest of the week Jim followed Kennedy Smartt around the outskirts of Atlanta and watched him share the gospel. Eventually, he too shared with people. He mimicked Kennedy's every idiosyncrasy. He began to sound like him as he asked the questions. He intoned, 'Do you know for sure that when you die you are going to be with God in Heaven,' with a southern drawl. He even slapped his knee as Kennedy had right before diving into the challenge to pray to receive Christ.

No one was exempt from hearing the gospel. They went into poor neighborhoods and rich ones. He saw a murderer accept Christ as well as an adulteress. Whole families knelt and gave their lives to God. Jim was astounded. So many lives had been changed that week, and his was one of them.

Who knew the 'professional evangelist' would be affected more than anyone else! On the way home he thought he might have to buy a bigger shirt. His heart was so full he was sure his chest had doubled in size. He could not wait to get back to Fort Lauderdale to try what he had learned down there.

20

WORKS EVERYWHERE

What if this presentation only works in the Southern Bible Belt. Sure, it worked in Atlanta, but who says it will fly in south Florida. The doubts swarmed in his mind. 'There's only one way to find out,' Jim said to himself.

'Anne!' he said when he arrived home. 'I've got so much to tell you. I can't wait to share my faith again.'

'I went to Atlanta as the teacher, but I was the one who learned the most. I wish you could have been a fly on the wall when Kennedy Smartt shared the Gospel.' The sun sank lower and their coffee grew cold as he retold the stories about the people in Atlanta who had trusted Christ. 'I want to try using Kennedy's presentation in Fort Lauderdale.'

'Oh, Jim! I knew it would be good for you to go to Atlanta. You are different from the man who left a week ago. It is evident that God is teaching you so much. When Moses met God on Mt. Sinai his face glowed. Yours is pretty close to high voltage.'

One month later, on May 22, 1960, Coral Ridge Presbyterian Church was recognized officially as a church. There had to be 50 full time communicants in order to earn this status. Jim stood in the pulpit and addressed the 66 members of Coral Ridge's congregation. He marked the people individually with a smile or a nod. He had shared Christ with almost everyone there and delighted in the salvation of each.

The Kennedys' new home was the church except for Sunday mornings. Anne set up folding chairs for evening services twice a week on their patio and prepared sack lunches in the kitchen for youth groups. Her mother shipped the family piano from Lakeland to meet the musical needs at their 19th Avenue home.

When Jim first began going out and sharing he did not want anyone to go with him. He was still a bit gun-shy after his first experience with the elder. However, he soon realized he could not reach everyone by himself and began to take men along to train them in evangelism. Vic Wierman was one. He went with Jim fifteen to twenty times before he finally got the courage to speak up and present the gospel to someone himself. But when he did he was amazed to see how receptive people were.

After a local doctor prayed to receive Christ with Jim, he was recruited to come along on evangelistic appointments. Dr. Freeman Springer went with Jim four times and became so excited about sharing his faith he went home to tell his wife, Dottie. 'You've got to go with me,' he said. The two of them went out the next night to call on one of his patients. When both the man and his wife received Christ, the Freemans were hooked and witnessing became a way of life.

Jim and Anne's date night wasn't the typical dinner and a movie. They preferred to talk to people about Christ. Anne shared the gospel with the wives while Jim spoke to their husbands. Ministering together not only knit their hearts and souls with each another, but also fastened them inexorably to Christ. A cord of three strands is not easily broken. This was the most exciting time they had experienced as a couple. However, the eighty hour work weeks wearied Jim. He would never be able to reach the city this way. He had to get help.

One morning as he prayed and read the Bible, he came to Jesus' great commission, 'Go and make disciples, teaching them to observe all things whatsoever I have commanded you.'

'I have gone and shared my faith Lord,' he prayed. 'I have been adding people to your kingdom one by one. But your Word says you are a God of multiplication. If I teach people to share their faith as Kennedy Smartt taught me and they teach their new converts to share their faith, the number of new believers will jump exponentially. You must want me to teach my flock to be fishers of men also.'

Jim knew he should develop a curriculum to follow if he taught evangelism classes. Before now, he had not paid much attention to what he said when he shared his faith. He began to make mental notes as he went out. Later, he wrote not only what he said but how people responded. He realized there was a pattern to his witnessing presentation. He put his notes into manuscript form and made copies for the upcoming classes.

On Sunday he made an announcement from the pulpit. 'Many of you have recently come to Christ and experienced the peace and joy of God. Don't you want to learn how to share that good news with others? This week we are beginning a six-week series to train you how to do it. We will start this Wednesday at 6:30 at my home.'

Jim lectured the group for six weeks. He began with two questions, 'Have you come to a place in your spiritual life where you know for certain that if you were to die today you would go to heaven?' and 'Suppose you were to die today and stand before God and he were to say to you, "Why should I let you into my heaven?" What would you say?'

Everyone enjoyed the classes and attended faithfully. On the last day Jim ended early in order for everyone to go door to door and practice what he preached. The results surprised Jim. He never anticipated the outcome.

Not one of his students went out to share their faith. Everyone went home.

'Maybe I should extend the classes to twelve weeks,' Jim told Anne the next day. 'I know I was completely unprepared to share my faith, and I had been to seminary. How can I expect these people to feel comfortable explaining the gospel with only six weeks of training.'

'Maybe so,' Anne agreed nodding thoughtfully.

Jim extended the classes to twelve weeks. He included more detailed suggestions on what to say and specific answers to objections which might be raised. At the end of the session the results were the same as those of the six-week training course. No one went out.

The next Sunday Jim announced they would conduct a twenty-five week training course. 'You will be completely prepared for anything,' Jim promised.

But even after such extensive training, no one used their new knowledge to tell their friends or neighbors about Christ.

'Lord,' Jim prayed. 'Why is this not working? I don't get it. Why will these people not share their faith? I have taught them everything I know and they just won't go. I know they want to go, but they are not doing it.'

One afternoon as Jim was driving to an appointment, he saw a young teenager driving along. A sign hooked on the back of his car declared in large bold letters, 'WARNING, Driver's Education.'

'That's it!' Jim yelled throwing a fist in the air. 'Thank you, Lord. How could I have been so blind? You do not teach a teenager how to drive a car by discussing it in a classroom. You get him behind the wheel and out on the street. Sure he needs the lecture, but the laboratory is essential.'

Jim grinned and nodded at the woman in the car next to him at the stoplight. She stared at him with a worried expression as if she thought he was out of his mind.

Jim waved and called, 'I am just talking with God!'

She averted her eyes quickly and fixed them on the traffic light. When it changed to green, she gunned her car and sped away quickly.

Jim thumped the steering wheel with his fist. 'I have got to get everyone out of the class-room and into living rooms!' He huffed in exasperation. 'Lord, how could I have been so blind?'

At the next training session Jim handed out addresses. 'Tonight,' he announced, 'we will be putting our training into practice.' He rubbed his hands together and grinned. 'This is going to be great. You will love sharing the gospel.' He linked himself with one group, Anne with another and the men he had already taught to the remaining people. Everyone prayed for God to guide them and provide people who were ready to hear the gospel. After two or three hours the teams returned to report what happened.

When everyone came back the excitement was thick and contagious. 'You will never believe what happened,' chorused several people in unison.

Jim stood. He laughed and held up his hands to quiet the buzz. 'I am glad you all enjoyed your time. We want to hear from everyone. Let us take turns. How about Anne's group speaking first.'

A young man jumped up and said, 'I'll tell what happened.' Then he shot Anne and their other partner an earnest expression. 'Do you mind if I tell?'

'Go ahead,' they said waving him on.

'We visited a couple from Kentucky in a condo.' He pointed toward the window in the direction they had traveled. 'They were enthusiastic when we told them what we were doing. They said they had just finished an intensive year-long Bible study with their pastor. But when Mrs. Kennedy asked if they knew if they'd go to heaven if they died tonight, they had not the faintest idea anyone could know such a thing.'

'They must have missed the whole point of the Scriptural study,' Anne said.

The man nodded. 'Yeah, I couldn't believe it. Anyway, both of them prayed to receive Christ.'

'Really! That's great,' Jim said, clapping his hands together.

'If I were the one talking to them, I would have assumed they were already Christians when they talked about studying the Bible with their pastor,' the young man continued, 'but Mrs. Kennedy didn't assume anything. She went on and asked the questions. I learned so much just listening to her.'

Anne reached over and grabbed his hand. 'When we go out next time you can be the one to ask the questions,' she said.

'I will. I'll never make assumptions again.'

'What about your group?' Jim gestured to Dr. Freeman.

'We visited a young woman,' the doctor said and turned to the lady sitting beside him. 'Maybe you should tell what happened. I did not see what you saw.' A blush crept up his neck to his cheeks.

The group laughed nervously when they saw his embarrassment and a couple of people shouted encouragement. 'Tell us!'

'Well,' his trainee said, with an awkward sideways smile, 'As Dr. Freeman went through the gospel with this woman, I noticed a pair of men's shoes under a chair. Since she said she lived alone I wondered whose they were. I had time to scan the room as Dr. Freeman talked and saw something else that seemed odd.' She bit her lip and paused to tuck a strand of hair behind her ear.

'What?' someone asked urging her on in her story.

'It was a pair of trousers – men's trousers.'

'No.'

'Yes! But what capped it off was the closet door cracked open three or four times.'

A burst of laughter exploded from everyone.

'I guess when we knocked on the door her boyfriend jumped into the closet without his shoes or pants.'

'We ruined his night,' the doctor said. 'When we finally left, he came out of his uncomfortable hiding place and had a new born-again Christian to deal with.'

As more and more people came to Christ, more and more people wanted to join the class and learn to share their faith with friends and neighbors. Jim had to come up with a name for his ground-breaking material. After World War II the population in the 1950's and the early 1960's increased exponentially. In America they called it the baby boom. Around the world it was called the population explosion. Jim thought the expression perfectly described the multiplication of the gospel mushrooming and accelerating in all directions. Thus the name Evangelism Explosion was coined. Little did he realize the far reaching repercussions his program would generate. Starting as a small ripple, it would grow into a tidal wave that would sweep the world.

21

PANICKY PASTORS

'The congregation has doubled in one year! We must get out of here before we burst the McNabb cafeteria at the seams,' said one of the church elders. 'Let's appoint a building committee to make preparations to build on the site we own off Commercial Boulevard.'

'I remember when I first saw the place,' Jim said. 'Nothing was out there back then. I said it would be a good spot for field mice to have church. The city has grown so much that now it is a perfect location for us.'

The building committee moved swiftly organizing a fund drive that netted $112,500. The church was a simple rectangular, single-gabled building of antique brick with vertical panes of tinted glass.

When Anne came into the finished building she grinned and hugged her arms. 'Brr, that air conditioning feels delicious. It's been so hot at McNabb school with only the ocean breeze through open windows. Our attendance should double when people do not sweat through the service.'

'It's so big,' Jim said, 'I hope our attendance doubles because we will be swimming around in all this space with only 250 people.'

'We have to make sure the nursery is ready,' Anne said, cutting her eyes sideways to look at Jim.

'Not only for the church,' he said grabbing her hand and squeezing gently, 'But for our home too. I can hardly wait.'

It wasn't much longer before they got the call they eagerly anticipated.

'It's a girl!' Anne cooed as she cradled the tiny infant.

Jim reached out and grasped one of the baby's tiny feet and jiggled it up and down. 'She's bowlegged,' he said with a crooked smile. 'Do you think she'll be able to walk okay?'

'Jim!' Anne said with a laugh. 'All newborn's legs look that way.'

'Oh,' he said and waggled her tiny foot. 'I didn't know that. But, I do know she is the perfect child we've been praying for,' Jim said.

Anne studied the tiny baby as if she could not tear her eyes away. 'She kind of looks like you,' she said, and turned so Jim could see the tiny face.

He kneaded his cheeks. 'I didn't realize my face looked so squished?'

'She's beautiful,' Anne said with a contented sigh.

Jim turned to the nurse who stood in the corner to give the new parents a bit of privacy. 'Excuse me,' he asked, 'where do we sign the adoption papers?'

On the line for the baby's name Jim wrote, Jennifer Lynn Kennedy.

As they drove home in their old Ford, Jim and Anne knew their lives had changed. The headlights shone through the darkness spotlighting the 5531 19th Avenue atop their black mail-box. Jim switched off the ignition and the engine tick-ticked, breaking the silence of the night. Jennifer sighed in her sleep as if she knew she was home. Jim draped his right elbow over the seat and leaned over to admire the little bundle in Anne's arms.

'You and me and baby makes three,' Anne sang quietly with joy in her voice.

'I can't believe it,' Jim whispered almost reverently. 'She's so tiny.'

'Let's show her to her new room,' Anne said. 'You carry her and I will unlock the door.'

Jim strolled up the sidewalk carrying Jennifer in the bassinet. He could not take his eyes off her. When he cooed baby talk, she kicked her tiny legs as if riding a bicycle. 'She's so fragile,' he whispered. 'I am afraid I'll break her.'

As Anne unlocked the door, Jim breathed deeply, savoring the fragrance of the night. He embedded this moment forever in his mind, a snapshot in his memory.

'I don't think I fully understood the great love our heavenly Father has for us, His adopted children, until now,' he told Anne. 'This tiny baby has entwined her little fingers around my heart. She is my treasure. It gives me a glimpse of the great love God has for me.'

The church doubled in size each year of Jennifer's early life. In her first year, they filled the new facility completely. By the time she was two-years-old, two services were needed to accommodate 665 members. During her third year, the church built an annex to the sanctuary. Membership topped 900.

Jennifer developed into a precocious little ball of energy. She loved listening to Bible stories, and she grasped their meaning. When she contracted chicken pox she moaned, 'Oh, Mommy, why did Adam and Eve have to sin?'

Anne covered her mouth with one hand to hide her smile. With the other she stroked Jennifer's fevered brow. 'I don't know, sweetie.'

From the pulpit Jim gave the burgeoning congregation his vision for the future. In a sermon entitled, 'You Can Change the World!' he laid out his goals. He declared the need for a Christian school offering pre-elementary, elementary, and secondary education. 'Coral Ridge can make it happen,' he said. He also envisioned a Reformed seminary that not only emphasized evangelism, but also reached the culture which was on a path of self-destruction. Jim wanted to set up evangelism training outreaches in every city, state, nation, and territory of the world as well as establish a twenty-four-hour-a-day FM Christian radio station and an international radio and television ministry to reach and teach the nations the good news of Jesus Christ.

A number of parishioners shook their heads in disbelief at their young pastor's plans. 'He is dreaming if he thinks we can accomplish all that,' several people were heard to say. But others not only caught his vision, they also became part of it.

It was about this time that Jim preached his yearly sermon on stewardship. 'There are many people who say, "I can't afford to tithe,"' he said from the pulpit, 'but if you don't tithe, you are robbing God. You are a thief and are bringing the curse of God upon your financial affairs.' Jim thought he had gone above and beyond God's call to tithe. He and Anne gave fifteen percent of their income back to God five percent more than the tenth God required.

He was unaware a president of a Christian college was in the congregation that day. Later in the week he received a letter from the man which said, 'I enjoyed your message, particularly your statement: "You can't out give God." I believe that and have been experimenting with it for the last few years. I have been increasing the portion of my salary that I have been giving back to the Lord's work by five percent per year. I am now up to fifty percent and am really looking forward to seeing what is going to happen.'

What an idiot. Jim thought. *I will tell you what will happen. You are increasing it five percent a year and you are up to fifty percent. In another ten years you won't have anything.*

Jim threw the letter aside making a noise of disgust in the back of his throat. He never answered it. However, like a gnat in his ear, it nagged him for several months. He could not help thinking, *Do I really believe I can't out give God?*

He knew he'd better face up to it, so he and Anne increased their giving, although not in the same way as the president of the Christian college. He was not patient enough to raise it incrementally, so he upped it in a chunk. The next year they gave twenty-five percent. He was amazed how God provided that year, above and beyond his expectations. The next year he increased it to fifty. Again God met their needs in amazing ways.

When Jennifer turned four, she had the run of the church. Most of the hundreds of members knew the pastor's pretty little daughter. She was bright and cheerful most of the time. But sometimes she reminded her mother of the nursery rhyme about the little girl with the curl in the middle of her forehead. When she was good she was very, very good, but when she was bad she was horrid.

Anne scowled down at her naughty child one day. 'Oh, Jennifer!' she said in frustration. Anne shook her head and raised her hands in the air. 'If you act like this now, how will you act when you're a teenager?'

Jennifer put a sticky little finger on the corner of her mouth and rolled her eyes heavenward, as she contemplated the secrets of the world. After a moment she brightened. 'Sufficient unto the day is the evil thereof,' she quoted in a childish lisp.

Anne stared wide-eyed. 'Where in the world did you hear that?'

'Daddy!' Jennifer giggled. 'Mommy you look so funny with your mouth open like that.'

Jennifer's fifth birthday was a landmark year for the church. Several additions had been made to the building on Commercial Boulevard, but they still could not keep up with the increase of new believers who flocked to the church. Traffic-stopping crowds lined the sidewalks before and after church on Sundays.

A driver in a passing car was heard to ask, 'What are they giving away in there?'

Jim consulted a friend and co-laborer in Christ, Bill Bright, founder of Campus Crusade for Christ. Bill came down to speak at Coral Ridge and Jim showed him their extensive campus. 'We are thinking of building another sanctuary over there,' Jim said, pointing across the busy street. We are going to purchase some more land down the street too. What do you think?'

Dr. Bright considered the question for a moment and then said, 'I think you are spreading yourself too thin. It will be dangerous to have people crossing this busy road to go to church then Sunday school. Why don't you consider buying some land somewhere else? That way you can start afresh and build everything together instead of spreading yourself up and down this city block.'

Jim heeded the advice and formed a search committee. In 1967 they snapped up ten choice acres of land facing east on Federal Highway, one of the principal arteries in Fort Lauderdale. It was not too far from the first church and comfortably within the boundaries of the familiar neighborhood. But it would be several years before they had enough money to build. The $676,000 purchase price for the land was an act of faith for the fledgling church which was only eight years old.

Coral Ridge was singled out as the fastest-growing church in the denomination and one of the most rapidly expanding in America. Jim was buried in a volume of mail from pastors across the country who wrote to find out the secret of his success.

Jim made an effort to respond to each letter, but doing so would become a full-time job. To solve the problem of explaining his evangelism method individually over and over, he decided to bring all interested parties to Fort Lauderdale and teach everyone at once. On February 20, 1967, Coral Ridge hosted the first Evangelism Explosion clinic for pastors. Announcements were sent out inviting ministers to Coral Ridge Church for instruction on this chain-reaction method of training. Before the pastors arrived, Jim gathered the lay people he had trained the previous years for a special meeting. 'Forty ministers have signed up to come to our first E.E. training for pastors. Who do you think should go out with them into the community when we have our day of outreach?' he asked.

The group stared at him blankly then began looking around the room at each other. One man raised his hand. 'These guys have all been through seminary. Why do they need someone to hold their hand when they go out sharing?'

A woman piped up. 'Surely you have some trained clergy to go out with the pastors.'

Jim grinned. 'You forget. I was –,' he crooked his fingers in the air pantomiming quotation marks, '"trained clergy" and didn't have any idea how to share my faith. You are going to train these pastors.'

'What! No way! You've got to be kidding! Us?' and a chorus of other protests punctuated the air.

Jim held up his hands to quiet their objections. 'Believe me, these guys are more terrified than you. Trust me. I need you to be my trainers. Everyone in here has taken someone through the course. Each one of you knows how to share the gospel. I am counting on you to help these men. They are no different from you. They put on their pants the same way. They are not super-spiritual just because they have been to seminary.'

The pastors arrived. All week, they attended how-to-do-it classes during the day. Each evening was spent with the church's lay witness teams for on-the-job-training. On the final night the visiting pastor on each team would be the one to present the gospel to the people they visited.

After the first night when the group gathered to share stories, one visiting pastor spoke up first. 'I'm the secretary for evangelism for my entire denomination,' he said. 'I heard about this new method and wanted to know more. Tonight my team shared the gospel with a man at our assigned house. He was not converted.' The pastor's speech hitched. He paused, looked down and wiped his eyes. Then he took a deep breath and smiled. 'But I was. I understood tonight for the first time in my life what it truly means to be a Christian.'

Spontaneous applause erupted in the room, and Jim strode over and faced him. The pastor laughed and brushed aside a tear. Jim gripped his hand, pulled him out of his chair and clapped him on the back.

A second pastor cleared his throat and said, 'I'd like to share something too. This morning I was angry about being here with all you nuts.' He laughed nervously. 'I don't know why I came, really, but here I am. I have been a preacher for seventeen years and tonight I have discovered I never really knew Christ. I watched two people kneel and give their lives to Jesus an hour ago. Nothing ...' he paused and swallowed hard to keep his emotions down, 'nothing has affected me as much as seeing the light come on in their eyes. I have been a bitter man.' He shook his head. 'But tonight I have given my life to God. I stand before you a new creation in Christ.'

Everyone surged to their feet and cheered in unison. The two pastors were herded together in the center of the group where Jim prayed for them and the people who had heard the life-changing gospel that evening.

Several visiting pastors stayed in the homes of their Coral Ridge trainers. On the last morning, when the pastors were supposed to share their faith, one of the hostesses went to awaken her guest. She knocked on the closed door. 'Breakfast is ready, Reverend.'

Silence.

'Reverend?' she called again.

Silence.

She knocked louder. 'Are you all right?'

She went to find her husband. 'Something is wrong. He is not responding. Maybe you should go in and make sure he is okay.'

Her husband knocked again, then opened the door, fearful of what he might find.

What he saw was totally unexpected. He laughed and called his wife. 'Come here. You have got to see this.'

She walked in and saw the empty bed. 'Where is he?'

'Look around,' her husband responded, sweeping his arm to encompass the room. 'He packed up and left. I guess he got cold feet.'

'You're kidding?'

'I guess pastors are scared to share their faith, too.'

'Too bad. If he had stayed he would have seen how simple it is. I was petrified my first time too, but I did it. It is fun now. If I can do it anyone can.'

That spring Jim met with Coral Ridge's church leaders. The men in the room were full of excitement about all the great things God had been doing. Jim cleared his throat and stood to speak. The buzz of chatter slowed and died as he began. 'Gentlemen, this has been an exciting time for our church. So many people have trusted Christ as their Savior and Lord. The church now has 1,339 members.' He paused while everyone applauded. 'All praise to God our Father, who draws men and women to Christ,' Jim said pointing heavenward. 'Now that the church is running so smoothly, it is time for me to do what I have always wanted since I first went to seminary.'

Everyone in the room went still. The quiet was palpable as Jim continued. 'I have always wanted to pursue my master's degree in theology. After finishing my graduate work in Atlanta, I was awarded a scholarship to the Chicago Graduate School.' He clapped his hands and several men jumped in alarm. 'I think now is the time to pursue it.'

No one moved. No one smiled. All faces stared from masks of stunned disbelief.

22

Gone North

Jim glanced left and right at the men who filled the room. Wide-eyed and slack-jawed, their expressions mirrored shock and dismay.

He raised his hands apologetically. 'I'll only be gone for the summer.'

'Oh! Ah!' The men collectively exhaled. 'We thought you were resigning.'

'No, no,' Jim said and chuckled. 'I did not intend for it to come out that way.'

In the summer of 1967, the Kennedys packed and headed for Illinois. Jim took his family on a tour of his old neighborhood. He pointed out his old apartment building. 'Wow! It's much smaller than I remember.'

'I don't think it shrank,' Anne said. 'You just grew up. Everything seems bigger to children.'

'I think it's big,' Jennifer said in her piping five-year-old voice. They toured the old football field where Jim's back pains originated. He recounted the story of how he got smashed and lost his memory.

'Did you really forget everything?' Jennifer asked.

'For the most part I only forgot the plays. But I was pretty confused. Now, I've got this pain as a constant reminder of those glory days,' he said, kneading his aching back.

They piled out of the car and strolled along the beach of Lake Michigan. The water stretched out and away till its edge met the horizon in a flat line.

Jennifer gasped and pointed. 'What ocean is this? Is it the Specific?'

Anne laughed, 'You mean the Pacific, and no, it is not the ocean. It is a lake, one of the Great Lakes.'

'I loved to come here when I was a little boy,' Jim said. 'In the winter the whole lake would freeze and we could walk on the water.'

'You could walk on the water like Jesus!' Jennifer gasped with wide eyes.

'No, funny girl. It would all turn to ice. Once even the waves froze. The wind whipped them into frozen volcanic mounds of ice. It was a fairyland.'

'Fairyland,' Jennifer whispered in awe and stared out at the water as if hoping to catch a glimpse of that other world.

'Your Uncle George and I came down to the beach and played on the frozen waves. It was great fun to dash up the sides of the ten-foot cones and jump over the top. Inside, a platform of ice sealed the structure a few feet from the top. But once, when I ran up the slope and leaped into the crater, something bad happened.'

'What happened, Daddy?'

'Well, when I jumped down I had thrown out my arms like this,' Jim held his arms straight out on both sides. 'And that was what saved me.'

'Saved you. Saved you from what?'

'A terrible death.'

'Oh, Daddy!' Jennifer gasped and covered her mouth. Her large round eyes peeped over her fingertips.

'Jim, don't scare her,' Anne chided.

'When I jumped over, my feet broke through the thin frozen platform. I hung by my outstretched arms on the lip of ice at the top while the dark freezing water churned below. I yelled and screamed because I was stuck. I had no way of getting out. My arms got weaker and weaker and I began to slip.' He made a motion as if he were about to fall.

Jennifer squeaked and bit her nails. 'Did you fall into the icy water, Daddy?'

'Just as I was about to slip into the dark hole someone reached down and grabbed me!' He snatched Jennifer up and hugged her.

'Eek!' she squealed, then broke into peals of childish laughter.

'Your Uncle George rescued me. And thanks to the Lord and your Uncle we are all walking here together today.' Jim set Jennifer down between Anne and himself. They grabbed her hands and she bounced along lifting her legs to be swung through the air every third step.

'I'm so happy,' Jim said. 'I remember lying on this beach and wondering what purpose God had for my life. Looking back, I see how He drew me to Him. Every step I took was divinely guided by my heavenly Father to prepare me for ministry and to bring glory and honor to His name.'

'Oh, Jim,' Anne sighed and snuggled in under his arm. 'I love being here with you.' They watched Jennifer sprint forward to chase a wave. 'It makes me so happy that we could come up together and visit your childhood haunts. This is going to be a great summer.'

As Jim kissed Anne, Jennifer ran to them and clasped their legs. She looked up with flushed and rosy cheeks. 'Hug me too!' When she grinned, her baby teeth flashed like little pearls.

A shadow crept along the beach as a dark cloud drifted across the sun. Anne shivered. She wrinkled her brow and glanced up shading her eyes as if something in the distance frightened her. Jim felt the hairs prickle on the back of his neck and a brief foreboding clutched his heart. But when Jennifer laughed and capered away he quickly forgot the moment of fear. He would later remember the moment and wonder if it had been a premonition of the pain that lay ahead.

Jim jumped back into the rigorous school schedule with both feet. The summer master's course crammed a year's workload into two months. The Chicago Graduate School was widely recognized for its challenging theology and Greek and Hebrew studies. Jim plunged in, setting his mind to absorb everything.

He had just gotten into the swing of school life again when he awoke one morning to find Anne sitting on the couch. With a yawn he walked to her. She watched him approach with the impassivity of a stranger.

He stopped. 'What's wrong?' he asked and his heart skipped a beat at the desolate expression on her face.

'I think I found something,' she said flatly.

'What? What is it?' He sat down and draped a protective arm around her shoulder.

With her left hand, she reached across her chest and probed her breast. 'There's a lump.'

Jim swallowed hard. 'Are you sure?'

'Yes, it's pretty pronounced. Feel it.'

Jim shook his head, vainly hoping if he did not touch it, the lump would cease to exist.

'Oh, Anne.' He kissed her temple and pressed her head to his chest. 'Father God, You have always taken care of us. You have always guided our every step and provided all we need. I ask you now to protect Anne. Don't let this be cancer. Please.'

On the advice of the seminary president, Jim drove Anne to a nearby hospital. He stood in the waiting room reading his Bible and praying for his beloved wife. On the way there, they dropped Jennifer at a friend's house. He closed his eyes and remembered her wave and call, 'I love you, Mommy and Daddy!' in her sweet high voice as they drove away.

He wondered if he'd wear a track in the linoleum as he paced the floor. When he had been in New York for the Arthur Murray competition, he had seen a caged tiger. The beast was the showpiece for a fitness center. It never ceased to prowl its limited space as it padded quietly back and forth on large dangerous feet, eyeing people as if they were steak on legs. He always felt sorry for that big cat. He remembered it now as he strode to and fro in the bleak hospital waiting room.

Surely, Anne will be fine. She is active and athletic. She is hardly ever sick. Jim shook his head. 'This is nothing,' he said to himself. 'I'm sure of it.'

At that moment the doctor walked in. 'Reverend Kennedy?'

'Call me Jim.'

'Jim,' the doctor said and paused.

This isn't good, Jim thought. 'What is it doctor?' he asked aloud.

'It's cancer.'

'Oh!' Jim stumbled backward and he fell in a hard plastic chair. The words slammed into him as a physical blow. A shooting pain shattered his chest. He clutched his heart with one hand and covered his eyes with his other.

'We have taken her straight to the O.R. They are prepping her for emergency surgery.'

Jim stared up at the doctor with wide eyes. 'Will she –,' he broke off. His mouth was dry. He swallowed with difficulty and tried again. 'Will she be okay?'

'We can't know until we go in. The best thing for you to do is go home and get some rest. It will take us awhile to operate, then she will be out of it the rest of the night. I don't want anything to disturb her.'

Before he left the hospital, Jim called Fort Lauderdale with the news of Anne's cancer. The church responded immediately. A twenty-four hour prayer vigil was held by the congregation to beseech the Lord to save her.

As Jim drove the forty miles back to the Chicago campus he found it difficult to see through his tears. He had difficulty breathing. Something large and heavy sat on his chest, crushing his heart and lungs. Darkness snaked into his soul as night fell, filling him with an unspeakable dread. He cried out to the Lord.

'Tis so sweet to trust in Jesus just to take him at His Word.' The words of a hymn poured into his mind.

'Just to rest upon His promise.
Just to know thus sayeth the Lord.
Jesus, Jesus how I trust Him.
How I've proved Him over and over.
Jesus, Jesus, precious Jesus,
oh, for grace to trust Him more.'

Jim sighed. The songs gushed in a torrent as if a fire hydrant opened to quench his burning soul.

'Praise God from whom all blessings flow.
Praise Him all creatures here below.
Praise Him above ye heavenly host.
Praise Father, Son and Holy Ghost. '

'I do trust you, Lord. You have always provided for us. I won't stop trusting you now.' The fear didn't immediately leave, but he replaced it with a verse or hymn whenever his mind would start running away. As if the Lord himself serenaded Jim, the songs in the night salved his raw heart.

The next morning he drove the forty miles back to the hospital to see Anne. She looked so small and frail in the narrow hospital bed draped with sterile white covers. Jim pushed a lock of her hair back and kissed her forehead. 'Hey, hon,' he said. 'How're you feeling?'

Anne croaked something, stopped, held her hand over her mouth and cleared her throat. 'I'm okay,' she said in a raspy voice. 'What did the doctor say?'

Jim averted his eyes. He fixed them on the window as if something outside had caught his interest. 'He said you are going to be just fine.'

'Jim,' Anne said, taking his hand and giving it a little shake, 'tell me the truth. I'm not a child that needs to be protected. I want to know.'

Jim riveted his eyes to hers. 'You have breast cancer,' he whispered.

Anne's eyes opened wide and her mouth formed an 'O.' Then she turned her face to the wall. A single tear coursed down her cheek. She reached up quickly and dashed it away.

'I'm okay,' she said when Jim reached out to reassure her. 'I guess it is always shocking to hear that word. Cancer,' she paused. 'You usually hear it in the same sentence with she died of....'

Anne looked wistfully at Jim for a moment, then her face brightened. 'How can I be sad. If the Lord wants me home, I'm ready to go.'

'But, I am not ready for you to leave,' Jim said, grabbing her hands and pressing them to his lips. 'Don't even talk that way. Everyone back home is praying for you. God is our healer. He will heal you.'

'Ahem,' someone cleared his throat at the door. Jim turned to see the doctor in his white lab coat. 'Excuse me,' he said. 'I just wanted to give you the good news. We believe we've gotten all the cancer. Mrs. Kennedy, you will be fine.'

Jim lifted his chin up and blew out a noisy breath. 'That is such a relief! Thank you, doctor.'

'But,' the doctor said, raising his hand to indicate he had not finished, 'she will be weak for a long time. You are going to school up here, Pastor?'

'Yes,' Jim nodded.

'And you have a young child?'

Jim nodded again.

'Do you have any family who might care for her while your wife recovers? She should not do anything physical for several months.'

During the time Anne spent recovering in the hospital she received many phone calls from friends. One afternoon, as Anne lay in her narrow bed, a knock sounded on her door.

'Come in,' Anne called.

A young woman peered around the door as if unsure she ought to enter. 'I am sorry for bothering you,' she said. 'You don't know me. I am the switchboard operator for the hospital.'

'Come in,' Anne said with a wave and smiled encouraging her .

The woman took a few tentative steps forward. 'I just had to meet you. So many people have been calling your room.' She looked down at the handkerchief she twisted in her hands. 'I do not mean to pry.' She looked up quickly. 'But I could not help hearing what you would say to people when they called.'

Anne felt a hot flush creeping up on her. She used her I.V. needle-laced hand to cover her neck. 'I-I am not sure what you mean,' Anne said with as much grace as she could muster. 'What have I said?'

The woman's face colored and she spoke quickly. 'Oh, I wasn't trying to eavesdrop. It was just that you are obviously very sick, but you are the one offering comfort to the people who call you.' She reached a placating hand toward Anne. 'I just had to come up and meet such an amazing woman.'

Anne bridged the gap as she took the woman's hand. 'I am glad you did. I do have comfort in spite of my diagnosis of cancer. It is because I know the Lord Jesus. He is the one who gives peace in spite of our circumstances.' Anne invited the woman to sit in the chair beside her bed then said, 'Can I ask you a question?'

The woman nodded.

'Do you know for sure when you die that you will go to be with God in Heaven?'

'Oh, I hope so.'

'If God were to ask you, "Why should I let you into My Heaven" what would you say?'

The woman's eyes widened. 'I have no idea. I have never thought about it before.'

Anne smiled and continued to explain to her how she could know for sure she would go to heaven when she died.

Anne's confidence in Christ was a living testimony to many other hospital staff. Following the example of Paul in prison, she used her confinement to share the Gospel with those around her. It comforted Jim to see her composure.

The three Kennedys had a very different summer than first anticipated. Jennifer spent her time with family friends who had children her age. Anne stayed with another good friend nearby and Jim spent most of his time in the library. It was lonely at first, but he threw himself into his studies, netting a 4.0 average in his courses.

One weekend he accepted a speaking engagement at a church in New York. Billy Graham was there too doing a large crusade and Jim was anxious to hear the great evangelist again. Several years earlier, he and Anne had attended one of his crusades in Florida. When the opportunity to meet Mr. Graham was offered, they had stood in line for an hour or more with hundreds of other pastors and their wives in order to shake his hand. The encounter lasted about thirty seconds.

'Hello, Mr. Graham,' Jim had said. 'I am Jim Kennedy and this is my wife, Anne. I am the pastor at Coral Ridge Presbyterian Church here in Fort Lauderdale.'

Billy Graham exhibited his famous smile with laugh lines crinkling the corners of his eyes. He grasped Jim's hand warmly, then Anne's. 'It is so good to meet you both.'

Then a dark-suited man had waved them on so Mr. Graham could meet the others in line behind them.

Jim sat alone in the first row of a metal bleacher in Madison Square Gardens reminiscing about his brief encounter with the man of God. When everyone around him stood to applaud, Jim looked up and saw Mr. Graham walking by with his associates. Jim stood also.

Suddenly, Mr. Graham stopped, turned around and retraced his steps. Jim thought he must have forgotten something, maybe his Bible. But he did not head back to the side entrance from where he had come, Billy Graham stopped directly in front of Jim.

He extended his right hand. 'Jim Kennedy!' he exclaimed.

Jim opened and closed his mouth a couple of times in astonishment before he found his voice. 'Yes. Yes, Mr. Graham.' He thrust his hand forward and grasped the evangelist's.

'How is Anne? I have been praying for her every day,' Billy said with a sober frown of concern.

'Anne! Oh, yes. She's doing well, sir. Thank you for asking. Thank you for praying.'

'Praise the Lord! I am so glad to hear it.' The lines on his face smoothed in genuine relief. He squeezed Jim's hand once, then turned and continued toward the podium in the center of the field.

'How did he notice me in this sea of faces?' Jim whispered to himself. 'How did he remember me when we met only once for a moment?'

The people around him stared with respect or awe thinking he must be a personal friend of the evangelist.

Not long afterward, Jim received a call from the Graham team asking him to present his unique outreach program at the school of evangelism Billy had started. Thus Jim began a thrice-yearly training program in conjunction with Graham's ministry.

At graduate school in Chicago, during the long months of isolation the summer of '67, Jim began to plot his master's thesis.

He wanted to organize his evangelism method into a working plan others could take and use as effectively as his church had. In the fall, the Kennedys returned to Fort Lauderdale. They were all glad to be back together in their own home. His first Sunday back, Jim stood in the pulpit and preached a sermon about his summer experience entitled, 'Songs in the Night.'

'In the midst of tremendous pain, grief or suffering,' Jim said, fixing his eyes on Anne's thin face. 'God gives us a certain kind of song in the night to carry us through shadows of the dark valleys.'

After church, Jim greeted his delighted parishioners. One older woman clasped his hand tightly. 'Young man,' she said patting his fingers with her soft wrinkled ones, 'You grew up this summer.'

Jim stepped back in surprise and chuckled. 'Well, thank you.' He wondered at her words and at first thought the older woman must consider anyone under 50 a mere youth. However, he and Anne discussed it later.

'I think what she meant is that people mature more when they undergo pain or grief,' Jim said.

Anne reflected and nodded. 'That is really true. Until you have been through a good bit of hardships you really have not grown up.'

For the next two summers the Kennedys moved north to continue Jim's studies in graduate school. In 1969, at the end of his third summer in Chicago, he graduated *summa cum laude*. He published his thesis that later became a bestseller bought and read by over a million people. *Evangelism Explosion* was the first of many books Jim Kennedy would author.

Jim missed his own graduation ceremony because it conflicted with Billy Graham's first World Congress on Evangelism. He and Anne traveled with several other evangelical ministers to Berlin, Germany for it.

While the men met and planned how best to reach the world for Christ, their wives were whisked away on a whirlwind tour of Europe. Anne had visited most of the countries with her sorority sisters after college but enjoyed returning as an adult. She took every opportunity to share her faith with everyone she came in contact with and found, to her delight, the Gospel was just as powerful and relevant to people in Europe as in America.

She was surprised that out of all the evangelists' wives, only one of her fellow travelers made efforts to spread God's Good News. Vonette, wife of Campus Crusade for Christ founder, Bill Bright, seemed to be the only one, besides herself, who carried the same torch as her husband.

Not long after arriving back in Fort Lauderdale, Trinity Evangelical Divinity School of Deerfield, Illinois, called Jim at Coral Ridge. 'In recognition of your outstanding achievement in the clergy, particularly in church growth and evangelism,' the man on the phone informed him, 'our school's board of directors has voted unanimously to confer on you a doctorate.'

Jim officially became D. James Kennedy, Doctor of Divinity. He appreciated the honorary sheepskin but had already set his sights on the real thing. It would take him nine more summers to complete his earned Ph.D. at New York University.

When the church board questioned his reasons for pursuing the degree he explained, 'Many people accuse Christians and ministers of being "uneducated ignoramuses" whose views on any matter are not worthy to be considered. The indication of academic degrees obviously silences this objection and hopefully removes a stumbling block on the part of some listening to the gospel.'

The summers in New York were a fun break for their family, but Jim didn't think the level of study at NYU as challenging as the three summers he had spent earning his master's degree at the Chicago Graduate School. One evening he confided in Anne. 'This secular university doesn't come close to the same standard I was held to at the theology school. They just have me jumping through hoops here. Every time I bring a paper to them the professors give conflicting arguments. First they say change this, then change it back to the way I already had it. They just don't agree with what I am saying so they are trying to find a way to discredit it. I believe they have forgotten the meaning of Ph.D.'

'What is the meaning?' Anne asked.

'Translated from the Greek it literally means 'teacher of the love of wisdom," he said with closed eyes, as if savoring the words in his mind.

23

MOVIE STAR

In the early seventies, America was embroiled in the Vietnam War. President Nixon had been in office only a short time when massive antiwar demonstrations were held in Washington, D.C. At Ohio's Kent State, protesters rioted, throwing rocks and hurling empty tear gas cans at National Guardsmen who had been ordered to contain the demonstration. The soldiers opened fire killing four students and wounding eight others. Along with the political unrest, a liberal New York abortion law took effect, making 1970 a bloody year for our country.

Hollywood responded with movies such as M*A*S*H, an irreverent film reflecting a liberal slant on war. Another was the tear jerker *Love Story*. It proclaimed Hollywood's twisted advice on relationships with the famous quote, 'Love means never having to say you're sorry.'

In 1970, Jim Kennedy was immortalized on the silver screen when *Gospel Films* produced a dramatic motion picture depicting the story of E.E. *'Like a Mighty Army.'* The movie chronicled Jim's struggle as a new pastor and his initial failure in evangelism. Its climax was the remarkable turnabout when he learned to communicate his faith, resulting in unprecedented church growth.

Although Coral Ridge had over 2,000 members on their roll, Jim was still very active in E.E. He faithfully went with his trainees every week to share the Gospel. One night Jim visited Dick, a young dentist, who embraced the Gospel wholeheartedly. Immediately after receiving Christ, Dick confided in Jim. 'Dr. Kennedy, I have been a member of a group in town. Have you heard of the Knights of the Round Table?'

'No, is it a jousting club?' Jim said with a grin.

'I wish it were. I am embarrassed to even tell you about it.'

Jim sat back and held his hands out with palms up. 'There is nothing you can say that will make me feel any different about you. In God's sight you are perfect because Jesus has given you his perfect record. He doesn't condemn you and neither will I.'

Dick looked down at the floor, but Jim noticed his embarrassment as a deep shade of red crept up the fellow's neck. Finally he looked up. 'I have to tell you. It will clear my conscience.'

Jim leaned forward and smiled in an effort to put him at ease. 'Go ahead.'

'The Knights of the Round Table is a terrible group.' Dick shook his head violently as if to expel evil images from his mind. 'I don't know how I wound up there. It has the appearance of an exclusive club with members clothed in tailored blue blazers adorned with a crest on the lapels. A friend invited me to join and I was glad to have the opportunity. They meet across town at the restaurant, The Round Table. However, the Knight's sole reason for existence is –,' he paused with his mouth open as if he couldn't think of the right word, 'is to, I don't know what to call it.'

'You're saying it is no civic group that meets to help the poor and needy.'

Dick snorted. 'That's the antithesis of what this club does. I guess if I had to sum the Knights of the Round Table up in one word it would be debauchery.'

'Debauchery?' Jim sat back, his brow knit in lines.

'Get drunk, get laid, get high. Name the sin of your choice and they specialize in it.'

'Whew,' Jim said exhaling with a low whistle. 'But you have to know, Dick, Jesus cleanses you from all sin. There is nothing God won't forgive except not accepting his Son.'

A tear slid down the young man's cheek and he flicked it away. 'When you explained that to me tonight, it was the best news I'd ever heard. I have been searching for God all my life. But I kept doing stupid things. I kept alienating myself from Him more and more. Finally, I thought I had reached the point of no return. I thought I was beyond redemption.'

'No one is beyond redemption. God longs for sinners to turn from their wicked ways and come to him. You are blessed to see yourself as a sinner. Many people I talk to think they are good folks. They don't realize no one is good enough to get to God. No one is perfect and that is what God requires. That is why he sent his Son, Jesus. No one can come to Him apart from Christ's sacrifice.'

'I am glad you came to my house tonight. Thank you so much.' Dick grasped Jim's hand and shook it fiercely. 'I have to tell you though,' he looked down at the floor and said, 'I'm afraid.'

'Afraid? Of what?'

Dick's eyes had a hunted expression. 'The Knights don't let people go easily. I am afraid they will come after me, and I will fall back into their lifestyle.'

'That's not a bad thing to fear. When a person thinks he is above a problem, he usually falls right into it. Let's get you plugged into a good Bible study. There are a lot of young people at Coral Ridge. You just need a new set of friends. Any time you feel you might be dragged back into your old lifestyle, call me.

I am available any time, day or night. Call me. We can weather this storm together.'

Jim enjoyed his new friendship with Dick who was eager to grow in his faith and called often to ask questions. However, one Monday Jim received a desperate call from the young man.

'They ambushed me. They tricked me. I didn't want to go. I didn't. I can't believe it. Oh, Dr. Kennedy, you have got to help me.'

'Dick, is that you? Calm down. Come by my office.'

'I can't come to church. I did disgusting things. God hates me.'

'No! Don't say that. It isn't true. There is nothing you can do to change God's love for you. You are his child. You may have gotten filthy, but his blood cleanses you from all sin – past, present and future. Please, come down and let's talk.'

Dick came to Jim's office. 'If we say we have no sin, we deceive ourselves,' Jim quoted 1 John 1:9. 'But if we confess our sins, God is faithful and just to forgive us our sins and to cleanse us from all unrighteousness.' He laid a hand on the unhappy man's shoulder. 'We all fail, but God is gracious. Ask His forgiveness. He won't turn you away.'

Through tears, the young man confessed his sin and expressed his desire to walk with God. But the Knights didn't stop their pursuit. A few weeks later they trapped him into coming to another drunken orgy.

On a Sunday night Jim received a frantic call from Dick's neighbor. 'Dr. Kennedy! Please come quickly.'

Two days later Jim stood next to a casket. It was closed because the funeral director could do nothing to cover the gunshot wound that took Dick's life.

Jim surveyed the small crowd who gathered for the funeral service. The front row was filled with young men. They sat with crossed arms and smug expressions chiseled on their faces. Wearing blue blazers with golden emblems on their right lapels, they looked as if they had stepped out of an advertisement for Brooks Brothers. The insignia, stitched in red thread, said 'Knights of the Round Table.'

Suddenly, seized with righteous anger, Jim swept a long finger at the club members. Towering above them like an Old Testament prophet he shouted, 'You!' then jabbed at the coffin beside him, 'are responsible for this young man's death. Dick tried and tried to turn his back on the filth and sin of your group. He sought to embrace a new life of virtue. But you jackals tracked him down and dragged him back into your den of iniquity. Because he couldn't rid himself of his so called friends,' he crooked his fingers symbolizing quotation marks at 'so-called friends,' then made a fist with his index finger pointing at his temple, 'he blew his brains out.'

Jim knew this indictment may not win him any friends or converts, but he was compelled to rain judgment where it was due. Little did he know one of those jackals would come back to bite him later.

When the director of the film *Like a Mighty Army* first came to Fort Lauderdale to meet Jim Kennedy, he stayed in a hotel by the beach. His first hours were spent basking in the Florida sun by the pool. In the course of the afternoon he struck up a conversation with a young man on a lounge chair next to him.

'You're from California?' the man seemed surprised. 'You've got sun there, why come all the way across the country to another beach?'

'I am a film producer and have come here to make a movie about a local celebrity,' the director responded.

The other man sat up and stared with admiration. 'That must be a pretty cool job.'

'It pays the bills,' he replied nonchalantly.

'Who are you going to make the movie about?'

'A pastor. His name is Jim Kennedy. Have you heard of him?'

The man leaped to his feet and snatched the sunglasses from his eyes. 'That man is an -,' he loosed a string of expletives.

'I can't believe anyone would want to make a movie about him. He accused me and my buddies of murder!'

The director sat up. This man's reaction had been quite startling and his defamation of Kennedy piqued his interest. 'Murder? Why was that?'

'I'm a member of the Knights of the Round Table. One of our members was involved in Kennedy's cult and the next thing you know, he commits suicide. Kennedy blamed us, but I think he is more to blame than anyone else.'

The director went to meet Jim with many misgivings. He wondered if he should mention his meeting with the man at the pool. He decided to test this pastor and see if he would try to defend himself. After the two sat down in Kennedy's office, the director said without preamble, 'I met a man at my hotel today who told me a few disturbing things about you.'

Jim's eyebrows shot up and he raised his palms. 'Tell me. I would like to know.'

The man twisted in his chair as if uncomfortable repeating gossip. 'I can't quote him exactly or you might excuse me from your office for blasphemy.' He went on to recount his conversation with the man by the pool.

'Well you know what the Bible says,' Jim said, when the director finished his story.

The man's eyes widened as if this was not the response he expected. 'What's that?'

'Woe to you when all men speak well of you.'

The director grinned. 'Good answer. I am looking forward to working with you Dr. Kennedy. You will have to tell me what really happened.'

A Hollywood actor, Chris Robinson, played the role of Jim Kennedy. The real Jim Kennedy hoped the false one would give his life to God. 'How can Chris tell this story and recite the Gospel without being moved to accept Christ as his Lord?' he wondered aloud after dinner one night.

'He says he is a devout agnostic,' Anne said, picking up plates and carrying them to the kitchen.

'I know, I had lunch with him this afternoon. He told me where they are filming is almost in the same spot where he was born.'

'Maybe he will be reborn in there too.' Anne handed Jim a wet dish to dry.

'He said it was the first time he heard a preacher who did not just talk about a blind emotional experience.'

'Sounds like God's got his number.' Anne grinned. 'Let's bump him to the top of our prayer list.'

After the camera crews finished their work, they went back to California. Chris maintained homes in Hollywood and Florida. While home at Boynton Beach, he continued spending time with Jim. They developed a close friendship, often sailing together and talking late into the night about spiritual issues.

Several months after the movie came out, Chris's wife accepted Christ in the Kennedys' living room. Chris held out a couple of weeks longer, then he too surrendered his life to God. Immediately, his life began to change.

He did not tell Jim right away but waited till they went sailing again. The water was rough and the boat mounted and dove through the surf as it was driven by a strong wind. It wasn't the atmosphere Chris would have chosen to tell his friend and mentor of his new faith. But when the boat plunged abruptly into a trough, Chris blurted, 'Jim! I have received Christ!'

The movie not only changed the life of one actor, but it also made an impact on many thousands. According to Billy Zeoli, president of Gospel Films, during the 70's and 80's, *Like a Mighty Army* was shown in more churches than any other film ever produced.

Coral Ridge celebrated 1971 with a ground-breaking cere-mony on Federal Highway along with the purchase of five more acres adjoining the site. Architect Harold Wagoner of Philadel-phia was engaged to design and build the worship center and church facilities. He was well known for his construction of the National Presbyterian Church in Washington, D.C., but it was his breathtaking design of the Air Force Academy Chapel at Colorado Springs that made him world famous.

Mr. Wagoner began by erecting a three-hundred-foot tower to anchor the church in front. The hollow-poured concrete form, thirty stories high, became Florida's third high-altitude marker between Cape Canaveral and Miami. The top ninety feet consisted of a fourteen-ton stainless steel spire and cross. An aircraft beacon that shone on the tip is known by many fishermen and boaters as a mariner's light.

Cathedrals and churches during the Renaissance were often built in the form of a cross with two arms stretched out on either side of a long nave down the middle. Wagoner updated the configuration with a contemporary design making the sanctuary symmetrical. Whatever is seen on one side of the room is almost matched by something similar on the other. When Jim and Anne stood on the construction site where the pulpit would be, Jim felt a twinge of awe. 'It's gigantic! How will we ever fill all 3,200 seats?'

Anne squeezed his arm. 'Remember what you are always telling me, "God always provides." He is doing great things here.'

Jim nodded. He quoted God's promise in Malachi, '"Bring all your tithes into the storehouse and prove me now, says the LORD of Hosts, if I will not open the window of heaven and pour out such a blessing that there will not be room enough to receive it." That wasn't only true in 400 BC, but for all times.' He looked at Anne and asked, 'Did I tell you I increased our tithe again?'

'Well, I should hope so,' she said giving his arm a playful slap. 'God has done so much for us. It is only right that we increase our giving. You have always said,' she lowered her voice to mimic his, "you can't out give God." How much are we giving now?'

'Seventy-five percent, and God continues to provide above and beyond all we need. Building this church isn't any different. I don't want this structure to be some kind of showpiece for D. James Kennedy. I want it to be a magnificent cathedral dedicated to the worship of the Creator of the Universe.'

Because of Jim and Anne's background and love of music, they wanted to make music an integral and important part of the worship service. Twelve lofts would surround the crown jewel of the sanctuary – a Ruffatti pipe organ. It was one of the largest European-built organs in the United States. With over 6,600 pipes, the smallest the size of a pencil and the tallest over forty feet high, it would make a powerful, joyful noise unto the Lord.

As the church began to take shape, a couple approached Jim in his office one day. 'Pastor, is there anything you particularly want to have in this new church?'

Jim did not have to think about it. He knew what he wanted. He had preached a sermon about the need for it a few years before. God was bringing his vision to reality.

'When I was a pagan, not even seeking God, He sought me. I never would have gone to church, so God used something I had in my own home to get my attention.'

The couple sat forward, eager to hear what amazing thing God used to grab the attention of the man who was now their preacher. 'What is it?' one asked.

Jim rocked back in his chair, steepling his fingers and grinned. 'Radio.'

'Radio?' they chorused.

'We can't make people come to church, but everyone in America has a radio. If we could build a station in our new sanctuary, we would have a megaphone through which to spread the good news of salvation to more people than we could ever reach any other way.'

The man stood up and extended his hand toward Jim. 'You've got it, pastor.'

24

RACE TRACK

In August of 1971, a painting of the Westminster Academy school crest was displayed in the back of the sanctuary. People gathered to admire the artwork. It featured a pair of lions separated by the sword of the Spirit, topped by the helmet of salvation and overlaid with the shield of faith. Not many realized Jim not only designed the logo, but also drew and painted it himself.

'I knew I would get some use out of those paints and brushes one day,' he told Anne earlier that day as they both admired his artwork.

'I was about to throw those old tubes away,' Anne said. 'You haven't had time to paint in a long time. I thought the oils had dried up.'

In the sanctuary, Jim stood before the families who gathered to celebrate the opening of the new school. 'Westminster Academy has been created for the members of our church. Our vision is not only to educate our children with excellence in every subject, but more importantly to instill a Christian world-view. However, my desire for the school is also purely selfish.'

He reached down and clasped his blonde nine-year-old by the shoulders. 'I really started this school for Jennifer, but you all are welcome to come too,' Jim said with a grin.

Because the facilities were still under construction when September rolled around, the new school began classes at Pompano Harness Race Track. It was an open-air facility with no walls to separate the grades into rooms. Teachers took creative license and used betting booths to split up the classes. Students sat at round tables and teachers made up word problems about harness horses and their drivers.

The Headmaster, Harry Miller, was also a minister at the church. The kids teased him about how his name hung over the lounge door since the beer sign, Miller High Life, blazed there in a neon glow. The lounge also served as music class. The school ambitiously registered students from kindergarten through grade eleven. Eight eleventh graders made a small group, but all enjoyed the novelty of a classroom that looked down on the bleachers and race track below.

At first the heat and flies were pestilential. Students began to kill the insects and line them along their desks as trophies. The race track was a unique place to hold the first months of school if you didn't count the skinned knees from the parking lot playground, the bugs, or having to close one week for a horse show. After September and October the racing season came into full swing and the small school moved into two local churches. Parents pitched in to help move from the track and set up the new classrooms. There was much laughter along with the work. Everything was so exciting and new and no one complained.

Jim took every opportunity to promote the new school from the pulpit. He and Anne were very involved in helping, often inviting individual teachers for dinner. One evening after dinner, Jim lounged on the floor with Jennifer and her fourth-grade teacher as they played a board game.

When Jennifer ran into the kitchen to help her mom, the teacher confided in Jim. 'I have to tell you Dr. Kennedy, when I knew Jennifer would be in my class I was a little concerned.'

'Oh?' Jim said.

'You know, I was thinking preacher's kids are always spoiled and want to be treated as prima donnas. But I have been fascinated to see how Jennifer fits in so well with the other kids. She does not expect preferential treatment and is always upbeat and positive.'

Jim slapped the floor and smiled broadly. 'That is just about the nicest thing anyone has ever said to me.' His eyes crinkled merrily. 'I often think we should have named her Joy instead of Jennifer. She not only brings her mother and me so much joy, but she has such a happy spirit.'

That night made an impact on the teacher. She would never forget it. The Kennedys weren't stuck-up and stiff; they were down-to-earth. Not only were they kind, they were also fun. She had not thought such a busy man would have time to play a board game on the floor with his daughter and her teacher, but he made the time. She was impressed.

On December 23, 1973, eight thousand people packed the new church on Federal Highway for its first worship service! Jim agreed with the Psalmist, 'It is good to go into the House of the Lord.'

Two months later, Billy Graham preached a dedication sermon from the new pulpit to 12,000 avid listeners. 'I hope this congregation will never forget it was born only a few years ago with 45 people who loved the Lord, believed in prayer and believed in evangelism. You have done something that has become a twentieth-century phenomenon in the kingdom of God.'

Not only did Jim study Scripture and doctrine, he also kept abreast of historical and current events. He was greatly influenced by the Dutch reformer Abraham Kuyper who was not only a pastor, but also a theologian, newspaper editor, and politician in the Netherlands. He also ran two newspapers, organized the Netherlands' first political party, started the Free University of Amsterdam, and served as Prime Minister.

His actions made a tremendous impact on the political and social landscape of the Netherlands for the next century. His writings shaped a school of thought whose influence has been felt around the world. He called all of society to a radical vision of faithfulness to its Creator.

Jim was convinced that the way Kuyper lived his life and the core of his theology should be a model for the church of our day. It demonstrated how to live in the world and transform it for the Kingdom of God.

During the middle part of the twentieth century, many Christians either turned toward materialism or separated themselves from society and politics. The latter was largely due to the belief of Christ's imminent return. These Christian separatists regarded the culture as a sinking ship soon to be evacuated. As many believers gave up their influence, secularists invaded.

Kuyper's writings influenced Jim to take a stand for righteousness in the culture. He began to preach the Cultural Mandate from the pulpit. 'Perhaps you have never heard of the Cultural Mandate. It is right there in the opening chapter of the Bible in Genesis 1:28. God says, "Be fruitful and multiply; fill the earth and subdue it; have dominion over the fish of the sea, over the birds of the air, and over every living thing that moves on the earth." We are stewards of the earth and accountable to the Lord God who made it. We must apply the teachings of God and His Word to the totality of life. We must get involved in our culture. Don't just curse the darkness – light a candle! We must all be dedicated patriots.'

As an avid reader, Jim knew the potential for persuasion that could be locked between the pages in books. After completing his best-seller *Evangelism Explosion* he set his pen to other tasks.

In 1973 alone, he wrote three books: *The God of Great Surprises*, *This is the Life*, and *Spiritual Renewal*.

The next year he wrote *Truths that Transform*; an in-depth presentation of basic Christian doctrines.

That fall another ministry was realized when radio station WAFG 90.3 FM was licensed by the FCC to Westminster Academy as a noncommercial educational station. Whether through print or on the air waves, Jim dedicated himself to knowing God and making Him known.

25

MISTAKEN IDENTITY

Jim never ceased studying. Not only did he pore over Scripture, history and current events, but he also analyzed communication. From the beginning of his ministry, he recognized the importance of speaking effectively. Each summer since seminary he had set aside time to learn the art of preaching. He hoped to paint Scripture pictures that would imprint themselves upon the minds and hearts of his listeners.

Among other things, he studied body language, voice inflection, humor, attention-getters and dramatics. Using the Roth Memory System, he committed whole books of the Bible to memory. In one sermon he quoted more than twenty minutes of a famous speech on the deity of Christ given by Napoleon Bonaparte.

With dedication to truth proclaimed with style, Jim's first televised broadcast was an instant hit. Coral Ridge Church began their Media Outreach Division known as CRM in 1978. Before beginning the television ministry, Jim conducted a survey asking what disturbed people most about Christian

T.V. The overwhelming response was, 'Those televangelists are only in it for the money.'

Because of this, Jim determined not to take a salary from any ministry he founded, including the television or radio programs. He refused the right to any royalties from books or materials sold on the stations. He also increased his tithe and gave 100 percent of his church salary back to the Lord. God continued to provide for the Kennedys above and beyond their needs through other means.

CRM grew quickly with weekly programs that combined worship services with interviews, field reports and human-interest segments. Jim never shied away from controversial issues. CRM researched and produced commentaries such as, *Pornography: An American Tragedy*; *Creation Science Special: A case for Creation*; and *AIDS: Anatomy of a Crisis*. These programs were filmed in different parts of the country not only for authenticity but also viewer interest.

Reviews were largely positive, but some people made it clear they did not agree with Dr. D. James Kennedy. One afternoon as Jennifer played tennis on the courts by the church, she saw a man drive erratically into the parking lot. He bounced his car over a curb and parked askew on the sidewalk. The engine ticked furiously hissing and spitting fumes as if gasping for breath. The man jumped out, clothed solely in denim cutoffs and wielding what looked like a club.

He marched toward the courts and banged the fence with the crude bat. 'Where's the lord of this place?' he grunted.

Unsure what 'lord' this guy sought, Jennifer pointed an unsteady finger toward the church.

As the neanderthal stalked toward the building, Jennifer sprinted to the side entrance to warn her dad. She arrived just in time to see him enter the reception area and bash his club on the secretary's desk. 'I want to see the lord of this place!' he demanded.

Before the startled woman could answer, the sound of sirens wailed in the distance. The man lifted his chin. His nostrils flared, giving him the appearance of a dog scenting the wind. Abruptly, he dropped the club and ran. Jennifer caught a glimpse of him stealing a bicycle just outside the door. He grabbed it, threw a leg over the top tube, and pedaled away.

Crash! Her father slammed the office door against the wall as he dashed from his office. 'Jennifer!' he exclaimed seeing his flushed daughter. He grabbed her shoulders with both hands and studied her face. 'Are you okay, darling?'

She nodded wide-eyed.

'Did you see him? What did he look like? Where did he go?' he shot out the questions in quick staccato.

'He's wearing blue-jean-cut-offs and that's it.' She made a slashing motion and grimaced. 'He ran outside, grabbed somebody's bike and took off.' Jennifer trotted after her dad as he followed the madman's footsteps. 'What are you going to do?' she asked.

Jim jerked his car door open. 'He said he wanted to talk to me. I'm gonna find him and talk. Which way did he go?'

'I think that way,' she pointed toward a road that led to the beach. 'Daddy!' she yelled as his engine roared to life, 'he took a ten-speed bike with some sort of green decoration on the front.'

With a clenched jaw, Jim nodded and pressed his wheezing Pontiac into the chase.

Sirens blared and Jim knew the police were responding. He zigged and zagged down narrow streets hoping to catch sight of the bike thief. But after combing the area, he concluded it was hopeless. The club-wielder must have either ditched the cycle or his head start enabled him to get away.

After searching the area, Jim slammed on the brakes and pounded the steering wheel with a fist. 'Rats!' he said shaking his head. 'I wanted to catch that guy.'

As he started to turn around and head back to the church, he saw something out of the corner of his eye. It flashed in the sun. He shielded his eyes and stared into the glare. Several blocks ahead a bicycle careened into the street.

Jim stomped the accelerator and launched forward with a speed that would have garnered a ticket had the cops caught him on radar. Sure enough, it was a man pedaling fast, clad only in cut-off blue jeans. Jim roared around the cyclist and screeched to a stop, executing a textbook police roadblock.

He leaped from the car, sprinted to the bike and grabbed the handlebars with the expertise of a matador refusing to be gored.

'Are you looking for me?' Jim asked. He felt the veins bulge in his neck as emotion coursed through him.

'Me?' the man squeaked.

'Yeah! You!' Jim jerked the handlebars with a vicious twist.

'I'm not looking for you, man.' The fellow lifted his hands as if Jim pointed a gun.

'Oh, yes you are,' Jim hissed through clenched teeth.

'No, man, really!' The man cowered.

'The police are looking for you.' Jim tilted his head and listened to the distant wail of sirens. He hated bullies and wanted this guy to know he could not come marching into church wielding a club at his secretary. He boiled when he thought of his precious Jennifer armed only with a tennis racket.

'If you want me, you better come to me. Not innocent women and children!' Jim jerked the handlebars again and the front wheel bumped against his leg. He glanced down. 'You want –,' he hesitated. A recollection pricked the back of his mind.

Something was wrong.

Jim stared at the bike.

'What did Jennifer say?' he mumbled to himself.

'I don't know any Jennifer, I swear!' the man protested.

Jim remembered. She had said the bike was a ten-speed with a green decoration on the front. Jim examined the bike and saw, to his horror, it was a beach cruiser, stripped down and rusted. It not only was not a ten-speed, it looked like one of those beach rental bikes.

Confirming Jim's fear, the man bleated, 'I am just here on vacation. I just want to go to the beach. Really, man, I don't want any trouble.'

Jim closed his eyes and wished he were anywhere else in the world instead of Fort Lauderdale, Florida, holding this poor tourist captive. He wondered vainly how to gracefully extricate his foot after he already swallowed it. He gave the handlebars a feeble pat and dropped his head hoping the man would not recognize his face if he were ever flipping channels.

'Just don't let it happen again,' Jim mumbled. He hurried back to his car, slunk behind the wheel and left the man who'd probably think twice before vacationing in this city again.

The police traced the real suspect's address from the license on his abandoned car. Upon entering his apartment they made a startling discovery. The man had evidently not liked what he had been watching on T.V. He had hacked his set in two with an ax. The handle jutted out of the splintered glass and wood of the television.

When Jim was told about the shattered television he laughed. 'I don't know what I was preaching about, but it sounds as if it convicted that fellow.'

Another unhappy customer showed up at church one day with a pistol in his belt. Angered that his wife and children had trusted Christ, this man, an alcoholic, decided to punish the one responsible. An alert usher saw him pull the sidearm out and proceed unsteadily toward the door of the sanctuary. Before the gun could be wielded against his pastor, the usher disarmed the man and muscled him out the door.

From ominous phone calls – 'Tell him he dies tonight' – to bomb threats and hate mail, nothing fazed Jim's commitment to speak truth.

'Blessed are you, when men shall revile you and persecute you, and say all manner of evil against you falsely, for my sake. Rejoice and be exceeding glad; for great is your reward in heaven.' Jim quoted Matthew 5:11 when anyone asked him if he feared these threats. 'I have learned to say with Paul, "In whatever state I am, to be content."'

26

BELLS RING AND ANGELS SING

'You knew this was coming,' Anne said patting Jim on the arm as he slumped over the dining room table his head cradled in his hands.

'I know,' he said with a heavy sigh. 'It just happened too fast.'

Anne sat back and stared out the plate-glass door at the wisps of clouds feathering across the blue sky. 'It did.' A tear welled in her eye then spilled over the edge. Anne did not bother blotting it away. She was not even aware of it dripping off her chin.

'Mom, Dad,' Jennifer said in a subdued voice. She laid a hand on her mother's shoulder interrupting her reverie. 'You okay?'

Anne looked up and saw the tracks of tears lining her precious daughter's cheeks.

Jim stood and clutched Jennifer in a close embrace. 'I don't think I can let you go.'

'I'm not sure I want to go.'

'You have to go,' Anne said as she wrapped her arms around both of them. 'Auburn is a great university. You'll forget all about being homesick once you are there.'

'No, I won't,' Jennifer said with a catch in her voice.

'It just happened so fast,' Jim said holding Jennifer back so he could study her face. 'Who is this woman? What have you done with my little girl?' He shook her gently.

'Oh, Daddy, you are such a goofball,' Jennifer's laugh hiccuped into a sob.

The long drive to the airport flew by too quickly as the three recounted stories and assured each other of their mutual love. At the gate Jim and Anne bid Jennifer a tearful goodbye. They knew it was the best thing for her to go, but none of them could hold back their sorrow of separation.

'I'll be back soon,' she called as she walked down the ramp to board the plane.

Jim and Anne waved until she disappeared down the throat of the loading ramp into the interior of the aircraft. 'Let's go,' Anne said. 'We can watch the plane take off from the beach by our breakfast spot.'

It was a short drive to the Irelands Inn where they had spent vacations with Jennifer when she was young.

'The usual place?' the maitre d' asked with a flourish and a smile as he ushered them to the patio dotted with several tables shaded under large green umbrellas. Anne sat down and picked up the menu, but Jim took the short flight of steps to the beach. As he stood on the shore and stared at the ocean, the tears broke through his reserve and flowed in rivers down his cheeks.

A low rumble sounding like a growl of hunger from a giant's belly vibrated the atmosphere. Jim felt it in the pit of his own stomach. He looked up and saw a plane flash in the sun as it climbed into the blue. He waved his arms frantically in a pantomime of a marooned sailor signaling a passing ship from his desert island. 'Jennifer! Jennifer!' he shouted, little caring what the beachcombers might think. 'I love you! I love you!'

From the cabin, Jennifer looked down on her rapidly shrinking playground. The water winked and waved below. It beat its breast against the sandy shore in a desperate act of frustration against its boundaries. As the plane rose, defying the laws of gravity, Jennifer could not stop crying. She thought breaking out of Fort Lauderdale to go to college would be freeing, but an ache of homesickness twisted and writhed in her chest. As she stared out the window, she hoped to see the hotel where she and her family spent so many happy hours, but the receding shoreline turned an unfamiliar shoulder.

Jim walked with a bowed head back up the steps to the patio where Anne waited and the eggs congealed into cold mounds. 'I'm not hungry,' she said with a grimace and shoved her plate back.

'Me neither,' Jim said and propped his chin on his fist. 'Our joy just flew away from home.'

'It seems like we brought her home from the hospital as an infant just yesterday,' Anne said with a sigh.

'It went too fast.'

'People have always said that, but I didn't understand what they really meant till now.' Anne reached over and grabbed Jim's hand. She squeezed it and smiled at him. 'It is a good thing we love each other so. I have heard of many marriages crumbling when the kids go to college.'

Jim brought Anne's hand to his lips and kissed it. 'I do love you with all my heart.'

It was not much later that Jim received a call from his dad. 'Hey Jimmy. I am heading your way and was wondering if you could pick me up at the airport.'

'Sure, Dad! What's the occasion? You know Jennifer has gone off and left us.'

'I knew she'd run away some day. There is only so much religion a person can take.'

'Dad, I was joking. She's gone to Auburn to go to school.'

'Auburn? That's the cow college in Alabama. Is she studying agriculture or veterinary medicine? Why didn't she go to one of Florida's fine institutions and stay near home?'

'Auburn has changed a bit in the past few years, Dad. She'll be studying nursing.'

'People or animals?'

'People.'

'Well that's a good thing. Maybe she can nurse me back to health. I am having some eye trouble and am coming to that specialty hospital down in Miami. Would you mind taking me over?'

'I'd love to.'

When Jim saw his Dad at the airport a few days later he was surprised at how weak he had become. As they made their way through the terminal, he huffed and wheezed as if climbing Mount Everest. 'Dad, are you okay?' Jim asked squeezing his dad's thin shoulder.

The elder Mr. Kennedy looked at his son with tired old eyes and tightened his lips in a flat smile. 'Well, Jimmy,' he said with a sigh, 'I am not doing so well.'

Jim threw his father's bag in the trunk, then helped him into the car. 'I love you, Dad,' Jim said as he drove out of the parking deck.

'I know, son. I love you too.'

'I love you so much I want to spend eternity with you.'

Silence.

'If you stood before God and He asked you, "Why should I let you into heaven?" what would you say?'

'Jimmy, you have asked me this a thousand times before.'

Jim nodded his head and glanced at his dad. 'I'll never stop asking you. To know God and experience his love and forgiveness in this life is the most amazing gift I could ever share with anyone. However, you could be standing on the precipice of eternity. I can't let my father go without doing everything in my power to urge you to embrace Christ as Savior and Lord.'

His dad sat rigid in the passenger seat for a moment. Then his shoulders sagged and he said, 'All these years you have asked me to trust in Christ. You have said in order to know God we must have faith. Faith!' he gestured feebly with his right hand. 'What is that?'

'Faith is the hand of a beggar receiving the gift of a king. I realized many years ago that I could do nothing to deserve eternal life with God many years ago. But I thanked God for sending Jesus Christ to pay the penalty for my sins and asked Him to forgive me. That is what it means to be saved by faith – to realize we need a Savior and receive the gift God has already given us in His Son. We may not see or feel any different. But faith is believing in what we cannot see. You had faith I would pick you up at the airport when you asked me. You didn't worry I wouldn't come. When we have faith in God we believe He'll do what He says. He will save us.'

'If that is true then why should anyone try to live a good life if all we have to do is ask God to save us?'

'The reason for living a godly life is gratitude. That's the motive for doing what's right. I am not trying to gain something I don't have by my efforts to be good; rather, I'm saying "thank you" for the gift of eternal life Christ has given me. A former president of Princeton put it this way in a book. He said as a young man he accepted Christ and the gift of eternal life. All the rest of his life was simply saying, "Thank You, Lord, for what You gave to me." The Bible puts it this way, "The love of Christ compels us."'

'I think I see. Everything you have said all these years is finally fitting together. I don't know why I have been so set against it.'

'Dad, you can receive Christ right now. Christ's perfect life and record is imputed to us the moment we believe. It is placed to our account so that in the sight of God we are reckoned as perfect. God won't hold your past against you. It is as though the spotless white robe of Christ's perfect character and obedience were placed upon us, and in that robe we stand faultless before God. Only in this way can we ever acquire the perfect standing that God requires. Would you like to stop trusting in yourself and start trusting in Christ?'

'Ahem,' his dad cleared his throat and sat up in the passenger seat. He turned his watery eyes on his son and nodded. 'I would.'

'When Christ comes into a life as Savior, He comes to do something for us; to forgive our sins and give us eternal life. But, He also comes as Lord. He comes as Master and King. He comes to demand something of us. He says there is a throne room in your heart and that throne is rightly His. He made you. He redeemed you. He bought you with His blood. He says that He wants to take His rightful place on the throne of your life. Are you willing to yield your life, to surrender your life to Him out of gratitude for the gift of eternal life?'

'I am.'

Jim swallowed hard and reached to hold his dad's withered hand. 'Why don't you pray with me, Dad. The Lord is here with us in this car.'

His father nodded and squeezed his hand then pushed it away. 'Ten and two son. Keep both hands on the wheel in all this traffic. I don't want to die before I receive Christ.'

Jim laughed. 'Okay, Dad. Will you pray right now with me.'

'Yes, I will.'

'God is looking at your heart more than He is listening to your words. He says, "You shall seek Me and find Me, when you search for Me with all your heart." Father in Heaven, I thank You for my dad, who through You, brought me into this world. Thank You that I have the privilege to be with him now as he comes into Your kingdom. May the Holy Spirit draw him to you. Give him faith to believe Your promises. Give him repentance to turn from his sins. Reveal to him Jesus Christ crucified today.

'Dad, just pray after me. You won't be talking to me, but to God.'

His dad cleared his throat again and said, 'Ready.'

'Lord Jesus, I want You to come into my life and take over right now.'

'Lord Jesus, I want You to come in and take over my life right now,' his dad repeated in a rough voice full of emotion.

Jim's voice broke as he continued, 'I am a sinner. I have been trusting in myself and my own good works.'

'I am a sinner. I have been trusting in myself and my own good works.'

'But now I place my trust in You. I accept You as my personal Savior. I believe You died for me,' Jim continued.

'I put my trust in You, God. I want You to save me. I finally believe You died for me.'

'I receive You as Lord and Master of my life. I turn from my sins and follow You.'

'I receive You as Lord and Master of my life. Help me to turn from my sins and follow You.'

'I accept the free gift of eternal life. Amen.' Jim finished leading the prayer and glanced at his dad.

'I accept the free gift of eternal life even though I am not worthy of it. And thank You God for my son, Jimmy, who never gave up on his old man. Amen.'

'Dad, if you died tonight do you know where you would spend eternity?'

'In heaven.'

'And if God asked you why you should be in heaven, what would you say?'

'I'd say my son helped me understand what Jesus Christ did for me and what it means to have faith. I'd say, I prayed and invited Jesus into my life to forgive me and be my Savior. That is why.'

Silence filled the space between them for a moment as the joy of the Lord crowded out all words. In Jim's mind bells rang, angels sang, and the Rufatti pipe organ played songs of rejoicing. He reached to hold his dad's hand again.

His dad squeezed it. 'Thank you, son.' he said with a crack in his voice then pushed Jim's hand back. 'Ten and two. Ten and two. Put both hands on the wheel. I don't want to die in a car wreck. This traffic is terrible.'

27

SALT LAKE TO SALTY SEA

'A prophet?' Jim said. 'No, I am not a prophet.'

'A visionary then?' the reporter said.

'I am an observer. I watch what's going on and see what needs need to be addressed.'

'Over twenty years ago you gave a sermon entitled, "You Can Change the World!" In it you laid out several goals for this church: to establish a Christian school, begin an evangelism-training outreach, start a radio and television ministry and establish a seminary. So far you have founded Westminster Academy, which writer and commentator Cal Thomas declared, "One of the finest Christian schools in the country." You have a twenty-four-hour-a-day FM Christian radio station and an international radio and television ministry. And your evangelism-training outreach is planted in every nation and territory in the world.

'So, Dr. Kennedy, you have met four out of five of your visionary goals. I would say that is pretty good.'

'God is good,' Jim answered and smiled. 'But you're wrong about one thing.'

'Oh?' the reporter said with a curious frown.

'Last May, of 1988, I met with Drs. Synesio Lyra, Paul B. Fowler and Dominic Aquila to discuss the need for a Reformed and evangelical seminary in South Florida. In September, I assembled a working committee to discuss and strategize the launching of a new seminary. We settled on several principles that, in our opinion, are essential for the school. We have already assembled our staff: Dr. Joseph Hall as Librarian and Professor of Church History, George Knight as Acting Administrator and Professor of Greek and New Testament, Dr. Robert L. Reymond as Professor of Systematic Theology and Apologetics and Dr. Douglas W. Culver as Professor of Hebrew and Old Testament. Next year, in June of 1990, I plan on retiring as Moderator of the PCA General Assembly and officially announce the formation of Knox Theological Seminary.'

'Whew!' the reporter exhaled and sat back in his chair. 'In just over twenty years you have accomplished every goal you outlined back in 1965.'

Jim shook his head and wagged a finger. 'No, you're wrong. I did not do these things. God did them. I just happened to be the vehicle He used to accomplish the task.'

In the first few years of its existence, Jim watched with pleasure the powerful seeds of influence the seminary sowed across the country.

'I am more of a fireman than a pastor,' Jim Dietz said to his wife, Becky, one afternoon. 'We have seen incredible things happen here in Brigham City, but there is a lot of heat.'

She nodded in agreement. 'I never knew till we moved to Utah how encompassing the Mormon church is. It is more than a cult. It is a way of life. The culture is dictated by their religion.'

'I have been pastoring twenty years now, but I need more guidance. These last ten years here have only shown me how much I don't know. I need solid doctrine to help me understand how to fight these spiritual battles.'

'Is there a seminary nearby where you could commute? I hate to think about uprooting our whole family for you to go back to school.'

'What about Kansas?' Jim asked. 'We could go back home and maybe I could get a part-time job in the church where I was youth pastor to help pay expenses.'

Several days later Jim called Becky from the church. 'Hey, Honey,' he said, 'how'd you like to go to the beach?'

'The beach? You mean by the Great Salt Lake?'

'The water is salty where I want to take you, but it is much bigger than the lake.'

'What? Did we win a free vacation to California or something?'

'Other coast,' he said, 'and not exactly a vacation.'

'What are you getting at?'

'I've been offered an 80 percent scholarship to Knox Seminary!'

'Great!' she gushed. 'That is fantastic. How far is the commute?'

'Three thousand miles.'

At first Jim thought leaving his job and moving to Florida was a little crazy. However, he soon found the long hot drive in the U-Haul to Fort Lauderdale well worth it. Coral Ridge made the transition easy for them. He was offered a full-time job teaching at Westminster Academy and attended classes part-time at Knox Seminary just across the street. Jim discovered a new level of learning he had never experienced before. He looked back on his previous twenty years as a pastor and saw his teaching had only been surface deep. *If only I had known this when I was a pastor*, he thought. *I could have strengthened my congregation and ministered to them in a much deeper way.*

Not surprisingly, he found Knox as strongly committed to the Great Commision as its founder. Training in E.E. was a vital part of his education, along with teachings on the Cultural Mandate.

Because of his experience, Jim Dietz decided to stay at Knox as a recruiter. He aspired to help other men and women see the value of understanding the depth and richness of Scripture before jumping into ministry and getting in over their heads.

When applicants call to find out about tuition and scholarships, Jim tells them about Knox's donor base of people who give generously to help students cover expenses.

Graduates with backgrounds ranging from pastors to fashion designers, ex-marines to morticians, have walked the halls of Knox. One congressional aide commuted from Washington, D.C., in order to better impact her sphere of influence for Christ.

Knox was the completion of Jim's vision of a training ground to transform men and women into ministers who in turn would transform their world. Many call him a prophet or visionary not only to have outlined his goals in 1965 but also to have seen the completion of every one of them. But Jim deflects the accolades by pointing an index finger heavenward to the Giver of vision.

28

STOP THE HATE

'The city commission just did it? The people didn't even get a chance to vote?' Jim stared at the phone as if it had grown horns. 'Unbelievable.'

'We need to get this on the ballot so the people can let their voices be heard,' the man on the other end of the line urged. 'I heard you speak on this subject on your last television broadcast. You are well-informed and speak more eloquently than I could on this subject.'

'I don't think the members of your congregation would agree with you. The name Charles Stanley commands instant respect,' Jim said. 'But I have studied this subject thoroughly. I'm sure everyone in Atlanta must be fired up about it one way or another.'

'That is putting it mildly. I'm sure you are aware it will take a large amount of money to get this bill on the ballot. And our opposition will be screaming that we are discriminating homophobics.'

'How are you planning on raising the money, Charles?'

'That is where you come in, Jim. Would you come to Atlanta to speak on this subject? I want the people of our city to understand what is at stake. We've reserved a banquet room in one of the downtown hotels to rally people to raise money for a plebiscite to vote against granting special rights for homosexuals in Atlanta. Why should they receive special rights as if they have some kind of disability?'

'I'd love to come. Let me check my calendar.'

'I've arranged for security to protect you while you are here.'

'Security? Do you think there is a need for that? Surely, there won't be any violence.'

'They shout for an unbiased opinion, but only when it is biased against them. They definitely have an agenda and are fierce against anyone who crosses them. It could get pretty ugly.'

'You said, "security for me." Aren't you going to be there?'

'Sorry, but I have a previous engagement in Europe.'

'Is the famous Charles Stanley skipping town instead of standing with the sheriff at high noon?'

'I'll be with you in spirit,' Charles said with a chuckle. 'This is very important and I do hate to miss it.'

'Sure you do,' Jim teased.

A few weeks later, when Jim pulled up in front of a tall hotel in Atlanta, he was shocked at the sight that greeted him. An angry mob of men and women shouted and screamed as they marched back and forth in front of the steel and glass edifice. Several waved signs with angry words slashed across the poster board. One read, 'The religious right is neither!' Another stated, 'Stop the hate.' Its carrier scowled and cursed at a couple entering the building through the revolving door.

'Hmm,' Jim said to the driver, 'Maybe these folks need to pay closer attention to their own slogans.'

He opened the car door to a chorus of boos and jeers. Several protesters spat at him. He ducked his head and hurried into the hotel. The auditorium was filled with the hum of low conversation. He was ushered to the platform and took his seat at the head table.

When Jim stood to share the call for Christians to uphold the Cultural Mandate, the hum of conversation ceased. Every person was riveted to his call for Christians to stand up and let their voices be heard. 'The relatively small crowd of secularists are screaming their propaganda and the world is listening. We must not sit idly by and watch our culture deteriorate. Homosexuals are not disabled. If they are granted special rights an employer would be required to hire them as he would a minority. Their agenda is to normalize their sin and anyone who disagrees is labeled as intolerant. But we see by the angry mob outside these doors who is intolerant of whom.' At the end of his passionate address, the room erupted in applause. Everyone stood to acknowledge their desire to reclaim their city for righteousness.

At the end of the meeting, Jim gathered his notes and the few items he had brought to the table. As he turned to leave, he ran into a wall of flesh. He craned his neck back with difficulty to glimpse the face that towered above. 'Give me your room key, sir,' a large African-American man said in a deep baritone.

'Why do you want my key?' Jim asked and took a step back to get a better view of this goliath.

'We need to retrieve your bags. We're transferring you to a different hotel.'

Jim glanced around the room at the plush surroundings. 'This one looks fine to me.'

The security man reached up and pulled his dark glasses down so Jim could get a good look at his eyes. 'The protesters outside booked every room on your floor.'

Jim stood straight and bowed out his chest. 'I've never run away in my life. I'm not afraid of them.'

'They are planning on throwing AIDS infected blood on you, Dr. Kennedy.'

'Here's my key,' Jim said slipping the white key card into the large hand.

His black guardian angel led him through the kitchen into long underground passageways in the bowels of the building. Finally, they reached what appeared to be a seldom-used entrance. The security man spoke into a radio, then cautiously opened the door. He removed the dark glasses and glanced left and right before taking Jim's arm and piloting him to the waiting car in the alley.

'I'll follow with your luggage later,' he said to Jim. To the driver he said, 'Take care of him,' and slammed the car door.

The dark sedan sped past the protesters who continued to yell at anyone who would listen. Their shouting had escalated into a fevered pitch. They had grown more vocal as the night progressed. Jim shuddered when he thought how much they must hate him. He looked back through the rear window and saw the sign, 'Stop the hate,' jabbing the air rhythmically to the shouted chants.

'I feel like I am in some kind of spy movie,' he said as his new keeper ushered him through the basement of the new hotel and into a service elevator.

'We have to take precautions, Dr. Kennedy. There are people out there who want to hurt you.'

Jim shook his head. 'Woe to you when all men speak well of you, for that is how their fathers treated the false prophets.'

'What's that?' the security man asked.

'The Bible says speaking the truth won't necessarily win you friends.'

'Why do it then?'

'I'm glad you asked. Do you have a few minutes for me to ask you a couple of questions?'

'Sure, I've got to wait here till they bring your bags.'

'What if you were to die tonight and stood before God and He asked, "Why should I let you into my heaven?" What would you say?'

The next morning Jim boarded the plane back to Fort Lauderdale. But when he arrived he was informed of another problem. 'It's your mom,' Anne said when she met him at the airport.'

'Is she okay?'

'Yes, but she just fired the woman you hired to stay with her.'

'How many has she fired so far?'

'I think this is the ninth.'

'I wish she'd come live with us or George.'

'Do you really?'

'Oh,' he exhaled. 'It would be difficult, but she is my mom. She hated the nursing home because she couldn't have free access to her drug of choice.'

'They look down on drunken belligerence in nursing homes.'

'She won't move down here and she can't get along with anyone we hire to help her. What can I do? She can't live alone.'

'Go see her, Jim. She needs you now.'

It hurt Jim to see his mother. She was painfully thin and her skin yellow and unhealthy-looking, but she opened her arms and cried, 'Jimmy!' when she saw her youngest child.

'Mom,' Jim said and hugged her. 'Did you fire this last woman so I'd come see you. You know all you have to do is call and I'll be here.'

His mother wrinkled her nose and pursed her lips as if smelling something foul. 'I never liked that last one. You picked her out, not me. She hid my – my –' she turned around and walked down the hall without finishing her sentence. Jim closed the front door and followed.

'Mom, why don't you come to Jesus? He is longing for you to give Him your heart.'

His mother leaned over the kitchen table and reached up to take Jim's hand. 'Sit down here with me, son. You've been telling me about salvation for so many years now. I even watch you on T.V. Did you know that? I've been running from God all my life. I've finally come to the end of my tether. I can't run anymore. Will you help me receive him now?'

221

Jim exhaled noisily. 'Wow, Mom! I can't think of anything I'd rather do more.' He squeezed her hand and smiled. 'Just pray after me. Lord Jesus –.'

A month later Jim's brother, George, and his wife, Chris, joined the Kennedys to lay their mother to rest. After the funeral Jim asked George if they could talk. 'Sure, Jimmy,' George said and sat opposite him.

'Both Mom and Dad made professions of faith one month before they died. Did you know that, George?'

His brother mumbled something indistinct and started to get up.

Jim held out a hand to stop him. 'Wait,' he said. 'You're my brother and I've got something important I want to talk to you about.'

George sat back in the chair and crossed his legs and folded his arms tightly across his chest. 'All right, shoot.'

Jim took a deep breath and plunged into the story of how he came to Christ. He started with the radio preacher who woke him with that startling question and continued through the whole E.E. presentation. At every pause or query, George didn't utter a word. He just grunted and shifted positions as if uncomfortable in his chair. Finally, Jim came to the end. He made an impassioned plea for his brother to come to Christ. He presented every angle of God's good news and shot down every argument anyone could possibly have against it. 'Well, George?' Jim asked.

'Are you through?' George said and leaned forward with raised brows.

'Yes,' Jim acknowledged.

'Are you *all* through?' He made a sweeping gesture with an arm.

'I guess so, unless you have any questions.'

George rose stiffly from the chair and walked out the door without a backward glance.

29

WASHINGTON OR BUST

'So, your mother listens to this preacher on the radio. Does that mean we have to join his church?' Frank Wright asked his new wife, Ruth, as they filed into the new member class at Coral Ridge Church.

'Sh.' She elbowed him and frowned. 'The pastor's right over there.' She shifted her eyes sideways and tilted her head at the man nearby. 'He'll hear you.' Ruth pointed to a couple of desks on the edge of the crowded room and they sat down.

Frank's eyes widened when he saw Dr. Kennedy chatting with a frumpy gray-haired woman in the front of the room. 'The pastor,' Frank said with emphasis. 'The pastor, himself, is teaching this new members' class?' Frank glanced down at the church bulletin he had picked up on the way in. He scanned the list of services the church provided and ministries it founded.

'Reverend Kennedy must be a very busy man,' he whispered to Ruth. 'He's written six books and has a radio and television ministry. I can't believe he takes time to talk with people who want to join the church.'

'He looks taller in person than he does on T.V.,' Ruth said.

'That's because our set is so small,' Frank shot back with a smirk.

'Welcome!' Jim spread his arms wide in a gesture that embraced everyone in the room. 'I'm glad you all have come tonight. I know you all have busy lives and I appreciate you taking the time to come to this meeting. As you can see, each of your desks has a three-by-five card. Please write down your answers to these two questions.'

He paused and waited for everyone to locate the cards and pencils for the pop quiz. He grinned for he never tired of making the inquiries that had become associated with his name – 'the Kennedy questions.'

'Have you come to a place in your spiritual life where you know for certain that if you were to die today you would go to heaven?' He pointed at the card of a woman in the front row. 'Write your answer on the card.' He watched as everyone began to scribble their ideas across the white rectangles.

'Okay,' he said and nodded when the scratching of pencils on paper had ceased. 'Now answer the second question. Suppose you were to die tonight and stand before God and He said, "Why should I let you into my heaven?" What would you say?' He acknowledged someone's grimace with a nod. 'Pretty good question, isn't it. Have you ever thought about this before?'

The man shook his head and began writing.

'All right,' Dr. Kennedy said and walked to a desk on the left side of the room. 'Everybody please pass your cards forward.'

'Are you going to read them out loud?' a woman asked with a nervous tone.

'Don't worry,' Dr. Kennedy assured her. 'I won't call out any names.'

When he had the stack of white index cards in hand, he thumbed through them, pulled one out and read, 'I think God would let me into heaven because I am a good person. I hardly ever sin. I rarely ever leave my house.'

Frank glanced around the room and wondered if the blue-haired old lady on the second row had been the author of that statement.

'All right,' Dr. Kennedy said with a hint of a smile. 'How good do we have to be to get into heaven? It says so in the Bible. Did you know that? Are you ready? Jesus says, "Be ye therefore perfect, even as your Father in heaven is perfect."'

'Perfect? Can anyone in here claim to be perfect?'

The blue-haired woman shook her head and Frank smiled inwardly at his guess.

'The book of James puts it another way: "If we offend in one point we are guilty of all." If we commit just one sin we step outside the realm of the law and become an outlaw. Just one bad thought, word or deed is all it would take to keep us from heaven.'

'Well, then no one's going to heaven,' said a tall man wearing blue jeans and a Rolling Stones T-shirt.

'It looks that way doesn't it? If perfection is the measuring rod God uses then nobody is going to heaven.'

Dr. Kennedy paused to let it sink in. When people in the room began to squirm, he went on to explain how God made a way for us to go to heaven and that way was through Jesus Christ, His Son.

After finishing his explanation of the gospel, Dr. Kennedy looked around at everyone. Frank squirmed in his chair as if he felt the pastor stared only at him.

'Some of you understand who Jesus is and why He came. You may have gone to church all your life.' Dr. Kennedy let his gaze rest momentarily on each person in the room. 'But you may miss heaven by eighteen inches.' He traced a line from his right temple to his heart.

'You have intellectual knowledge, head knowledge, but you have never asked Jesus to come into your heart and be your Savior and Lord, Master and King. You don't have a personal relationship that governs everything you do in life.'

Frank's Adam's apple bobbed up and down as he swallowed hard with an audible gulp. That night he went home and asked Jesus into his heart. Immediately, he and his wife Ruth plugged into the church. They not only grew personally in their faith, but reached out to others by taking the E.E. training where they learned to communicate the good news to others.

One Sunday in 1984, Frank Wright's eyes were opened to Dr. Kennedy's far-reaching vision of the future. The year before President Reagan spoke to an audience of 1,200 at the Association of Evangelicals in Orlando, Florida. While at that conference, he delivered the now-famous speech in which he stated, 'Let us be aware that while they (the Soviet Union) preach the supremacy of the state, declare its omnipotence over individual man, predict its eventual domination of all peoples of the earth, they are the focus of evil in the modern world.'

Both the United States and the Soviet Union had super-power status during the 1980's. Since World War II, the two countries had been involved in an arms race for power. Controversy arose over the Soviet Union's pursuit of détente in Europe, yet military expansionism persisted in the third world. By establishing a diplomatic presence in the third world, the USSR would gain access to a country's population in hopes of spreading its socialist theory.

President Reagan made a strong stand against this expansion declaring, 'In your discussions of the nuclear freeze proposals I urge you to beware the temptation of pride – the temptation of blithely declaring yourselves above it all and label both sides equally at fault, to ignore the facts of history and the aggressive impulses of an evil empire....'

Jim Kennedy had also been watching the Soviet Union. He was aware the arms race had become increasingly expensive for the Soviet Union, and as a result the Soviet economy had declined dramatically. While the rest of the world increased at a rapid pace in developing technological advancements, the Soviet Union was in a threatening position of being left behind.

Their standard of living began to fall and shortfalls in agriculture caused unneeded food shortages. The Gross National Product had rapidly declined from six to five to four and had fallen all the way into negative numbers. Although many in America feared the USSR and the arms race, Jim was convinced otherwise.

In 1984 he made his famous prediction before his congregation: 'Though I am not a prophet nor the son of a prophet, I believe there is every possibility that by the year 2000, Communism will be a thing of the past. And this specter, as Marx Engels described it, which has haunted Europe and now haunts the whole world, will have been exorcised from this planet once and for all ... the claws and teeth of the Communist bear will be extracted, and that hulk, that carcass, will be swept by the arm of God onto the garbage heap of history and hundreds of millions of people will rejoice.'

The congregation was stunned. Frank Wright shook his head and wondered how Dr. Kennedy could make such a declaration in front of so many people. He would be humiliated if this did not come to pass.

In the following years, Dr. Kennedy noticed Frank's commitment to Christ and his zeal to serve in the church, and offered him a job on the church staff. The congregation had reached a membership of around 7,000 by 1985, and the needs of the members were many and varied. Frank took over the job of community service. Through this ministry, the church demonstrated the love of Christ toward the community of Fort Lauderdale and surrounding areas by helping anyone in need. Community service is a practical way of being Christ-like. Through it people were clothed, fed, visited when sick, and consoled when lonely as dictated in Matthew 25:35-36.

For the next ten years Frank helped teach E.E. clinics that trained pastors in evangelism. Coral Ridge had not ceased to have pastors from around the nation who desired to be trained in Evangelism Explosion. Three times a year the church hosted pastor clinics. Dr. Kennedy always taught these along with several others he had trained through the years. Frank not only coached pastors in these clinics, he also traveled worldwide to teach E.E. to ministers in other countries.

Even when he entered graduate school to study for his Ph.D. in finance, Frank continued to work as an E.E. trainer. Dr. Kennedy had come to treasure their friendship and recognized him as a man committed to excellence. Two weeks after Frank graduated from the doctoral program, Dr. Kennedy came by to see him.

'Frank, or should I call you Dr. Wright now?' Jim said with a grin.

'You can call me Dr. Wright if you want me to call you Dr. Kennedy,' Frank shot back.

'Okay, then, Frank, I have a proposition for you.'

'Oh?' Frank raised his brows and asked, 'What is it?'

'I'm not sure if you've been aware of it, but last fall I initiated a planning committee to discuss the possibility of starting a new ministry.'

'You're starting another ministry?'

'I never stop praying and asking God how we can better spread His Gospel and influence our culture. I've watched Washington, D.C., for a long time. It is a place of enormous influence. It could easily be called the capital of the modern world.'

Frank nodded. 'I can see that.'

'If we reach the influencers of our government for Christ, then teach our congressmen and senators to walk with God, they would fulfill God's righteousness in our nation. I would love to see this country come back to the Christian roots on which it was founded.'

'That would be marvelous indeed,' Frank interjected.

'I'm glad you agree,' Jim continued. 'Because this is my proposition. I have watched you grow in your faith since you came to Christ in the early 80's. Since then you have proven yourself not only faithful, but also a man of vision and character.

I can not think of anyone else who would be more perfect to be the new Executive Director for the Center of Christian Statesmanship in Washington, D.C.'

'There's a Center for Christian Statesmanship?' Frank asked.

'In name only. You will be the one to begin it.'

'Dr. Kennedy, I am flattered. But, I've just finished my doctoral degree in finance. Are you asking me to throw it away, uproot my family and move to D.C.?'

Jim raised his hands and leaned forward. 'Never would I ask you to throw your degree away or suggest you accept any proposal that I or anyone else may give you. I only ask you to pray about it. And,' he said with a twinkle in his eyes, 'it won't hurt to have doctor in front of your name in Washington.'

Not long afterward Frank showed up in the Capitol with only a briefcase, business cards and checkbook. He began searching for a suitable building and workers to staff the new ministry. One of the first things he did was make contact with the few ministries that were making an effort to reach out to the Capitol. Frank helped these ministries form a partnership to work together and complement each other in their specific niches.

The year he arrived, Congress had 73 newly-elected members. Fifty of those were born-again Christians. Many of these Christians had heard D. James Kennedy preach either on television or by radio and were open to Coral Ridge's new ministry. The interest of these freshmen Congressmen was a great launching pad for Frank. He was able to establish five Bible studies right away for the congressmen and their staff.

Frank communicated his goals and plans for the Center of Christian Statesmanship with Dr. Kennedy and his board members. He immediately saw why Jim had been so successful in the ministries he had started. Speaking to his wife after the meeting he told her, 'I think one of Dr. Kennedy's greatest strengths is to give people a task then give them a free hand to design the ministry.'

'What did they think about your plans and what you have done so far?' Ruth said.

'They loved the Geneva Study Bible idea. You know, the R. C. Sproul Bible we gave to every member of Congress with their names engraved on the front.'

'I know.' Ruth nodded. 'That's the one that has the commentary and notes in the margins. It highlights scripture and Biblical texts that speak about the important issues designed for people in government. Who wouldn't love that Bible?'

'Evidently some of the congress members didn't. We got several Bibles back in brown wrappers.'

'You're kidding? Did they write a note to say why?'

Frank shook his head. 'Nope. But we were able to make appointments with most of the members. We tried to see every one of them, but were turned away by a few. I am finding more and more that everything in D.C. has to do with name recognition. We're running a full page ad in Capitol Hill's newspaper, *Roll Call*, tomorrow. I think that may open some doors for us. I have just been feeling my way along this year through trial and error.'

Ruth gave him a reassuring hug. 'I don't see much error. I think you are doing a great job.'

Frank hugged her back. 'I could not do it without you. You have been such an incredible wife. You are so supportive in every way.'

During the second year of the Christian Center for Statesmanship the world was rocked with an incredible announcement. All the networks carried the breaking news and every person would remember where they were when they first heard the broadcast.

Frank sat in his living room glued to the television. A blonde reporter held a microphone in her hand and gestured to a large gray wall behind her. 'The border between West Berlin and East Germany has a total length of approximately 103 miles. As you can see it has a deeply-staggered system of barriers.' She pointed these out behind her. 'The wall is made of concrete segments about thirteen feet high. There is an illuminated control area (also called death area) on the eastern side. Refugees who reach that area are shot without warning. A trench prevents vehicles from breaking through.' She pointed to her right. 'You can see the patrol track over there. The corridor is usually guarded by watchdogs. Over there are the watchtowers and bunkers, then a second wall.'

She turned back to the camera. 'Over 100 people were shot and killed here at the Berlin Wall. The last was only months ago, on the sixth of February this year – Chris Gueffroy.'

The reporter had to shout into the microphone because of the crowd surrounding them. The camera flashed away from her and fixed on a young man delightedly taking a pickax to the top of the wall. 'This,' the reporter stepped back in front of the lens and gestured at the screaming crowd, 'symbolizes the destruction of twenty-eight years of abuse to freedom.'

The masses began to form into mobs. Police were just standing around, watching with impassivity. The young man with a pickax was joined by others with sledge hammers. They succeeded in carrying away a nine-foot slab of the wall. Everyone shouted, cheered and clapped in a cacophony of noise.

From the East German side came the sound of heavy machines. They were punching holes in the wall with a giant drill. Every time a drill poked through, everyone roared. Fireworks, emergency flares and rescue rockets streaked across the black sky. Many used hammers to chip away at the wall. There were countless holes. At one place, a crowd of East German soldiers looked through a narrow opening. Hands reached through and clasped hands from the other side. Someone brought the reporter a chunk of the wall. She turned it over in her hand and held it to the camera. 'It appears to be made with cheap brittle concrete.'

Everything was out of control. Police on horses just watched. There was nothing they could do. The crowd swelled. Long alpine horns were blown making a loud huwoo. The wall was breaking. Cranes lifted slabs aside. East and West German police traded caps. People climbed up onto the wall and were sitting astride. When the final slab was moved away a stream of East Germans poured through. People applauded and slapped their backs.

The camera panned the crowd revealing tears and grins of indescribable joy. 'Do you speak English? Do you speak English?' the reporter asked as she shoved her microphone into the onrushing faces. Several jabbered back in every language from German, French and Polish to Russian.

A knot of people cheered as the mayors of East Berlin and West Berlin met and shook hands. Several East German guards stood watching with rifles slung over their shoulders. The reporter asked one of them, 'Do you speak English?'

The man nodded and grinned into the camera. 'Hello,' he said in heavily accented English. He crooked his fingers in an awkward wave.

'Are there bullets in those things?' The reporter gestured at the rifles.

The soldier grinned. 'No bullets.' He held the gun up for the camera.

From a house near the wall, someone set up loudspeakers and played Beethoven's ninth symphony. Thousands of people dotted the rooftops. Berlin was out of control. The police and the army were helpless. The soldiers were overwhelmed. They became part of the crowd. Their uniforms meant nothing. The Wall was down! A revolution occurred before the eyes of the world via television.

Frank laughed and hugged his kids. 'Remember this moment,' he told them, 'this is history.'

He turned to Ruth and said, 'Do you remember what Dr. Kennedy said?'

Ruth frowned. 'What he said about what?' she asked.

'He predicted this.'

'What do you mean, he predicted this?'

'Just after we joined the church he said before the year 2000 Communism would be a thing of the past. I thought he was crazy. But look!' he gestured at the television. 'It's happening!'

30

First and Last Doubts

'You've got to try it, Dad! And Mom, you'd love it too,' Jennifer gushed. 'It would be a fun family activity. We can go while I am out of school on winter or spring break. I have been with my friends several times. I'd love for our family to do it together.'

'You've already got us rollerblading,' Anne said. 'Even though everyone thinks sixty-year-olds have no business speeding around on in-line skates. I don't think we can take up another one of your hobbies. Besides we are from south Florida. Our blood is too thin for cold weather.'

'Right, Mom. I have seen you in New York. You weren't shivering too bad up there.'

'That's because we always went in the summers when your dad was finishing his doctorate,' Anne said.

Jennifer bounced on the couch, 'Skiing is so much fun! You don't know what you're missing.'

It wasn't much later that Jim watched a television special about snow skiing. The program, along with Jennifer's enthusiasm, finally convinced Jim to drag Anne to the colder climes. They would try out this sport their daughter was hooked on.

As in everything that caught Jim's attention, he studied the art of skiing from every angle. He read books and magazine articles on skiing and watched how-to videos. He was the most educated beginner on the slopes. He and Anne took lessons and shared Christ with every one of their instructors. 'Maybe I'll start a new snow ski ministry,' he quipped. 'You have enough time to go through the whole Gospel on the ski lift.'

'The family that plays together stays together,' could have been the Kennedys' motto. Snow skiing became one of the many outlets they enjoyed as a family.

After Jennifer graduated from Auburn, she moved back in with her parents and commuted to work at the hospital nearby. 'Nurses don't dress the way they did in the olden days,' Jim teased her about her work clothes.

'Weren't all the nurses nuns when you were little?'

'No, but they wore these cute hats that kind of looked like a nun's wimple. Do you know the history of the nun's habit?'

'Dad, you know what I love and hate about you is that you know so much about everything. I don't have time this morning for a history lesson. I've got to run.' She kissed him on the forehead. 'Bye, love you.'

Anne came through the front door from her morning walk just as Jennifer was leaving. 'Love you, Mom.'

'Bye, honey!' Anne called in return.

The telephone rang and Jim got up to answer it. 'Isn't it good to have her home?' he called to Anne.

Anne nodded and wiped sweat from her forehead with her T-shirt and stretched a bit as Jim picked up the phone. The cheerful 'hello' froze on his lips, the color in his cheeks drained, and his smile changed to a frown. 'I'll be right there,' he said after a long pause. 'I'll catch the next plane up.' He stopped again and listened. 'Okay, but call as soon as you find out where they're taking him.'

'What?' Anne asked when he hung up. She grabbed his arm as he sank into a chair. 'What happened? Are you okay?'

Jim looked up with wide eyes. 'He played tennis on Friday, worked out on Saturday and just stopped by the doctor's today because he had a nagging cough.'

'Who did?'

'My brother.' Deep lines of sorrow wrinkled his brow and his voice broke when he continued. 'He only has six weeks to live. They're transferring him to one of the two hospitals up there. Chris will call when she knows which one they will take him to.' Jim grabbed Anne's hand. 'We've got to pray for him. He will go to hell if he dies without Christ.'

'Lord!' Jim prayed. 'Save my brother. Your brothers did not believe you were the Christ the Son of God until You returned from the dead and appeared to them. You know the anguish of losing a loved one. Jesus, make Yourself real to George. Give me one more chance to share Your salvation with him.'

'I'm so glad Chris knows the Lord. This has got to be hard for her to have her husband's life hanging by a thread. It is so sudden,' Anne said.

'I remember how she accepted Christ in our front yard,' Jim said. 'I just wish she could have influenced George to become a Christian. We need to keep her in our prayers too.'

Jim drove to the church to tie up some loose ends in order to fly to Jacksonville to see George. He prayed continually as he moved from project to project. When he came back home Anne turned to him with sad eyes. 'Chris called,' she said.

'Where have they taken him?' Jim asked as he walked to his room to pack his bags.

'He's gone.'

'I know. He's leaving that hospital and they're taking him to another one.'

'No, Jim.' Anne laid her hand on his back.

Jim turned and faced her.

'He's gone. He died.'

'What!' Jim said stepping backward. 'He can't be. He just went in this morning. He played tennis on Friday. I prayed that

God would let me talk to him – give him one more chance to accept Christ.'

Anne slipped her arms around him and laid her cheek against his rapidly beating heart. 'I couldn't believe it either.'

On the plane to Jacksonville Jim complained to God. 'You have always provided. You have always guided me. You have never let me down. I have prayed for my brother for thirty-five years. How can you let him die without giving me one more chance to talk to him? Why? That wouldn't have been so difficult would it? Just a few more hours. You are God after all. Life and death are in Your hands.' He sighed heavily. 'I've never let anything bother me, Lord. You have always been there for me. You have always answered my prayers. I just can't believe it would be Your will for George to go to hell. Not after I've prayed for him for so long.'

When Jim arrived, Chris met him with red-rimmed eyes as if she had been crying a long time. However, she smiled broadly when she saw Jim. He didn't feel like smiling and wondered how she could, considering her husband was burning in eternal damnation. 'Jim,' she said. 'There is someone I want you to meet.'

'I don't really feel like talking to anybody right now,' Jim said in a grouchy tone.

Chris didn't seem to notice his edgy manner. She took him firmly by the elbow and led him like a dog on a leash to a young man who fidgeted nervously in the corner.

'Hi, Dr. Kennedy,' he said. 'It's an honor to meet you.'

Jim nodded and forced a half-hearted smile.

'I am the new pastor at Mrs. Kennedy – uh, not your wife – ah,' he cleared his throat. 'I mean your brother's wife's church.'

Jim nodded and looked away. His neck ached from his old football injury and he reached back to massage it. 'I am not feeling so good,' he said.

'Tell him, pastor,' Chris encouraged the young man.

'Your sister-in-law called me,' he nodded at Chris, 'and asked me to come talk to Mr. Kennedy, your brother.' He wiped the palms of his hands on his pants with a nervous gesture. 'We talked a while. He told me about the conversations you had with him and asked me a few clarifying questions. He evidently understood the basic gospel but had been angry at God and unable to give his life to him.'

Jim forgot his back pain. He stood straighter and stared intently at the young pastor.

The young man grinned and continued. 'After we talked a bit, I asked if he wanted to pray with me and ask Christ to forgive him and come into his life.'

'Did he?' Jim whispered.

'Yes, sir.' He nodded vigorously. 'He sure did. Right in the hospital room.' He jerked his thumb over his shoulder and grinned.

'Oh, Lord,' Jim bowed his head and prayed silently. 'Forgive me for my pride. How could I have thought I was the only one to bring George salvation.'

'Dr. Kennedy?' the young pastor asked. 'Are you okay?'

'Yes,' Jim said with glistening eyes. 'Thank you, son. Thank you so much for going to see my brother. God has taught me a lot today. I'll never doubt Him again.'

31

RECLAIM AMERICA

'We are America! We are America!' An army of 500 angry men and women yelled at the people who walked from their cars into the doors of Coral Ridge Church. Shaking fists and thrusting signs spattered with slogans, they marched up and down the sidewalk outside the sanctuary. A woman with spiked hair shouted, 'Bringing fundamentalist extremists here to "Reclaim America for Christ," is a threat to democracy and diversity.'

The air vibrated with rage. Tension was palpable outside the church.

Inside was a different story. (Sanctuary – sanc•tu•ar•y – a place of refuge or asylum.) More than 1,700 people stood with eyes closed praising God. Godly men and women taught those gathered inside how to reach America for Christ. Melodic strains of patriotic music moved the group mightily. It was a celebration – an invigoration. It was a call to awaken Christians and motivate them to action.

'We are not exclusive,' Vice President Dan Quayle said from the platform. 'We are inclusive.' He made a gesture that included the protesters outside. Quayle recalled the words of Ronald

Reagan, 'Our agenda is simple, but it won't be easy.' Quayle's commonsense ideals listed prayer, political participation (beginning with registering to vote), outreach, local involvement, and learning to seize short-term opportunities while 'preparing for the long haul.'

The gay and lesbian protest outside attracted media attention and even a counter-demonstration by a small collection of 'skinheads.' But it made little impact on the conferees who reacted with pity, not hate, toward the marchers.

Inside, Dr. Kennedy said much the same. 'Before God, I don't hate anyone. I pray for those who are chained by sin to be delivered and emancipated from Satan's deception.'

One of the church staff confided, 'I have often seen Dr. Kennedy take protesters to lunch. He walks out there and invites two or three to go out with him. He buys their food and talks to them about God's love then brings them back. And you know what they do then?' He smiled and answered without waiting for a response. 'They pick up their signs and continue marching.'

'I never expected it to be that good!' That post-conference comment typified reaction to CRM's first Conference on Reclaiming America held January 21-23, 1994 in Ft. Lauderdale. More than 1,700 people from across America attended the three-day event at Coral Ridge. The reason? To learn how to impact contemporary culture and reclaim America for Christ.

'The neat thing about this conference is that there was a practical call to arms,' said Elizabeth Hall, who, with her husband Robert, attended from Jackson, Tennessee. 'It was a multitiered call: to evangelism, to ministry, and to storm the gates of hell in our culture.'

Critics leapt at the phrase 'reclaiming America for Christ,' which proved the flash point for the protesters. A protest organizer told the *Ft. Lauderdale Sun-Sentinel*, 'What these people are doing is to try their best to codify into law their version of the Bible. And nothing could be more scary toward a democracy than that.'

Dr. Kennedy forcefully issued a 'call to arms' and responded to media criticism. He said in his 'Spiritual State of the Union' message: 'It's time to reclaim America for Christ, and I say that without apology. The one thing secularists want from Christians is their silence. We have been all too willing to acquiesce. Let us be silent no more.'

The conference was such a success it was repeated the next year. In the 1995 conference one theme stated that political action alone will not change America. 'Who gets more of your attention every day,' asked Kentucky State Senator Tim Philpot, 'Jesus or Rush Limbaugh?' And syndicated columnist Cal Thomas warned that 'even the noblest political causes can be a form of corruption when they distract our attention and effort from Christ's work in the world.'

'Once a year is not enough,' Jim told the CRM board members after the 1995 conference. 'People are awakened. They are moving. They are hungry. Although a feast is good, eating a meal once a year won't stave off starvation. We need to provide a regular diet of information that will enable these Christian soldiers to march onward as unto war. It will be an uphill battle to win this nation back to its godly heritage.'

'What are you proposing?' a board member asked. 'We have the Center for Christian Statesmanship in Washington. Is that not enough?'

Jim shook his head and frowned. 'No. Reaching the lawmakers is only half the battle. We must raise up a grass roots army and encourage them not only to spread the good news of God's salvation, but also to get involved in their country. For too long Christians have sat back and not taken action while our opponents have been working overtime. Using media, pornographers, homosexuals and abortionists have desensitized the public. Only a few years ago homosexuals were considered sexual deviants; now they are teaching it as an alternative lifestyle in sex-education classes in our public schools. The word incest was a horror, but in San Diego there exists a Childhood Sensuality Circle which contends that incest is a healthy practice. In the 1960's the idea of 'kiddie-porn' was criminal, but today it is exported to us from Holland in volumes. We must educate Christians as to what is going on. We must equip them to reach their cities, counties, states and nation.'

'Yes,' the board members agreed in unison, applauding to show their support.

'How can we do that?' one asked. 'And where, D.C.?'

'Not Washington. Here, in Fort Lauderdale. I propose to add the Center for Reclaiming America to Coral Ridge Ministries.'

On July 4, 1996, the Center was established. Its four-fold mission included: an Information Network to enable believers to report back to the Center on challenges to faith or religious liberty in their community; a Telecommunications Link to serve as a rapid-response device, urging Christians to pray or contact their elected leaders; a Christian Alert Bulletin offering 'culture-war' updates from across America; and an office of Traditional Values-based Legislation to draft model laws for introduction and passage in the states.

Dr. Kennedy tapped Pat Gartland, former chairman of Georgia Christian Coalition, to direct CRM's new Center for Reclaiming America. Gartland built the Georgia Christian Coalition from 300 members into an organization of 6,000 activists during his three-year tenure.

Although numerous organizations were involved in the fight to return America to her Biblical heritage, Gartland believed much remained to be done. 'There is such a need for information to get to the grassroots, and it hasn't been addressed,' he said. 'There are a lot of people who have not been touched or informed.'

The Center for Reclaiming America raised an electronic army of a half million. The Center provides these men and women with nonpartisan, non-denominational information, training, and support. It enables those interested to positively affect the culture and renew the vision of our Founding Fathers. Their website *www.reclaimingamerica.org* is a fountain of information offering many resources that inform, equip, motivate, and support the endeavors of the Christian activist. It includes:

News Stories that provide constituents with up-to-date and accurate information so that they can stay abreast of current issues.

Center Alerts provide regular information to the Center's rapidly growing E-Army. It can mobilize dedicated Christians to take necessary and appropriate action at a moment's notice.

Grassroots Training educates and enables Christians to make a positive impact in their communities.

Local Impact Tools equip participants to engage in the culture of communities. They provide step-by-step instructions and proven tips for becoming a church liaison, starting an Issues Awareness group, and engaging in other effective activities.

Reclaiming America For Christ Grassroots Training Conferences offer concerned, committed citizens an opportunity to learn grassroots training techniques from the experts. It combines proven action plans with real-life examples to create a uniquely inspiring and preparatory experience. Attendees are guaranteed to return home with the understanding, information, and training necessary to start making a difference – and to train others to do the same.

Fast Facts are packed with valuable information and statistics that address today's hot issues.

Christian Alert Bulletin provides an opportunity for churches across America to keep their congregations informed. It offers useful nuggets of information and a 3-minute action point each month.

America Adrift provides a monthly review of news from the front lines of America's cultural war.

National Prayer Force offers Christians a list of globally important matters to pray over. It offers constituents an opportunity to make prayer commitments for various lengths of time.

Pastors' Page offers valuable tips and resources to pastors, including sermons, legal guidelines for political activity, and a link to Evangelism Explosion training.

Online Bookstore gathers helpful and important literature in one easily navigable location. These resources can help people become more informed and effective leaders in their community.

Nothing highlights the Center's efficacy better than the 2004 presidential election battle between Bush and Kerry. The large majority of Republican 'red states' sent a strong message that Americans care deeply about family values and Christian principles.

32

ALL CREATION SINGS

'You can't teach at that school,' Tom's wife said.

'Why not, Linda?' Tom asked, 'I've been teaching in public schools and at the community college for nine years. I'm ready for a change. This private school won't have all the political bureaucracy the public school has. I am tired of fighting that losing battle.'

'I thought your friend set up a job interview with AT & T.'

'Teaching is my true passion. Besides, it couldn't hurt to go to Westminster Academy for an interview,' Tom said as he blew out a cloud of cigarette smoke.

'I thought I asked you not to smoke in the kitchen.' Linda grimaced and waved the white vapor toward the open window. 'Don't you get it?'

'I'm sorry,' he said and stubbed the butt in an ash tray. 'I'm just so agitated about this job thing.'

'I'm not talking about your nicotine habit. I'm talking about Westminster Academy.'

Tom raised his hands and shrugged. 'I don't see why you keep going on and on about it. It is just a school.'

'It is not just a school. It is the Coral Ridge Presbyterian school. It is James Kennedy, that activist pastor's, school. You are not even a Christian. Your religion is evolution. Do you think they will let you teach that there? They will want you to say God created the world in a week and then doused it with zillions of gallons of water in a universal flood that destroyed everything but a man and his zoo.'

Tom rolled his eyes. 'Nobody really believes that.'

'Well Mr. Brooklyn, New York Catholic, what did they teach you in seminary?'

'Don't go there,' Tom thumped the bottom of his pack of Camel cigarettes with the heel of his hand. A slim white stick of tobacco popped out and Linda grabbed it.

'No smoking in the kitchen.'

Tom closed his eyes and breathed deeply as if to calm his nerves. 'I did go to Catholic seminary, but knew I couldn't take the vows of poverty, obedience or chastity.' He raised his brows with an alluring look at his bride of four years.

'Well, I have to say I am glad. If you had taken that vow we wouldn't have our 2.1 kids so we don't contribute to the overpopulation of the earth.'

'Don't make fun of it. You know that is a danger. If we don't act responsibly, we are just part of the problem.' He sighed. 'I love teaching science. I just can't stand to be in public schools any longer.'

Linda wrapped her arms around Tom and hugged him close. She spoke over his shoulder in a soft reassuring tone. 'You are a great teacher.' She emphasized great with a squeeze. 'And you have the awards to prove it. Your book on the science fair has practically made you a household name.'

Tom held her at arm's length and looked carefully into her brown eyes. 'Are you on drugs?'

She slapped his shoulder. 'Ha, ha, very funny. Well,' she grinned, 'I may have exaggerated a bit. But not about what a great teacher you are. You are the best.'

Later that day Tom sat in Westminster Academy's Headmaster's office. He drummed his fingers on the arm of his chair, uncomfortable without a cigarette between them. His hand kept straying to his pocket where the pack nestled. He crossed and uncrossed his legs several times while Dr. Ken Wackes looked over his resume. It was the one he had prepared for AT & T. He mentally chided himself for not rewriting it to suit the school job. He looked at his watch and hoped he could get out of here quickly. This was wrong. All wrong. Why had he come?

Dr. Wackes looked up at Tom and smiled as if he read his mind and made an effort to put him at ease. 'Well, Mr. DeRosa, your resume is stellar. I appreciate your coming in for this interview.'

Tom nodded and shifted in his chair. 'No problem.'

'Whenever we meet potential teachers we explain Westminster's mission.' Dr. Wackes sat forward and struggled to pull something from his back pocket.

For a moment Tom's imagination supplied what the headmaster reached for.

A tract.

A stick of gum.

A gun.

He wasn't prepared for what Dr. Wackes pulled out and held before him. He opened his thin leather wallet and extracted a dollar bill, leaned over and held it out to Tom.

'Uh,' Tom said philosophically.

Dr. Wackes grinned. 'I'd like to give this to you.'

Tom stared at the bill and a frowned in confusion.

'It's free.' The headmaster waggled the dollar encouraging Tom to take it.

'O-kay,' Tom dragged out the word and reached uncertainly for the money.

'It's a gift. I know it's not a huge gift, but it is a good picture of what God does for us.'

Oh, no, Tom thought. *Here comes the sermon.*

'I'm not going to preach at you,' Dr. Wackes said, and Tom wondered if the man really could read minds.

'I want to give you a gift to illustrate how God gives. He gives us something we could never get unless it is freely given. No matter how hard we work or struggle to reach heaven, the gap between us and it cannot be bridged in any way. So God kindly gives us a way to come to him. But there is a catch.'

'I was raised Catholic. I understand all about rules and regulations of religion.' Tom said guardedly.

Dr. Wackes shook his head. 'I am not talking about religion. I am talking about a relationship. That is what God offers – a relationship with him. He wants to adopt us into His family.'

'What's the catch?' Tom asked sitting forward in his seat, the dollar clenched in his fist.

'What did you have to do to make that dollar your own?' Dr. Wackes asked, nodding at the money.

Tom opened his hand and stared at the crumpled bill. Absently, he straightened it as he thought about the question. 'I am not sure what you mean,' he said, and met Dr. Wackes' intent gaze.

'If someone gives you a gift, do you then need to work for them for compensation?'

Tom shook his head.

'Would you offer to pay them back later?'

'That would be an insult,' Tom said.

'What do you do when someone gives you a gift?'

'I guess you accept it and say thanks.'

Dr. Wackes struck his desk with his fist. 'Yes. And that is exactly what God did. He sent his Son as a gift to pay for everything we have ever done that blocks our relationship from Him. God said, "You can never be good enough to live with Me because I require perfection. But I want you to be with Me, so I'll send my Son to die in your place so you may live eternally with Me in heaven."'

On his way home from the interview, Tom drove by the hospital where he worked to put himself through graduate school. His years as a patient relations coordinator flooded back in waves of memory. Faces filled with grief and trauma rose before him as if he relived moments of tragedy with the families of the dead and dying. He recalled how the smell of gasoline assaulted his senses when the jet crashed in the Everglades. Torn and dismembered bodies lined the hospital hallways along with those who clung tenaciously to life.

Frantic people flooded in to find their loved ones. 'Are they here? Are they okay?'

He had to answer questions, soothe nerves and deliver the tokens of the deceased to their relatives. Even then he saw a stark difference between the grieving. Some wailed in despair while others quietly said, 'It's okay because he's with the Lord, now.' Tom wondered at the polarized responses. He had ditched his own faith years before at Florida Atlantic University.

Evolution was espoused in the classrooms not as a theory, but the only view anyone with half a brain could embrace. When challenged on Adam and Eve and Noah's ark, Tom's faith crumbled. He decided it was all a bunch of silly children's stories. If the world had no Creator it logically followed that religion was a fallacy propounded by the weak-minded to explain the world. Therefore the Bible was obviously false.

But he remembered being unnerved at the hospital when he had stared into death's sightless eyes. *What will happen to me when I die?* he wondered. No matter how much he discounted religion as the opiate of the feeble-minded, he had a hard time reconciling oblivion after death.

As soon as he got home that afternoon, Tom called his wife at work. 'You'll never believe it,' he told her.

'Are you smoking in the kitchen?'

He stumped out the cigarette. 'No.'

'I heard you exhaling.'

'Just listen. I've got something to tell you.'

'What is it? Are you okay?'

'I'm not sure. Gravity has been reversed in my world. I'm upside down.'

'Do you need to come in to the hospital for an EKG?'

'No, I'm speaking metaphorically. This man at the school talked to me about God and it made sense! For the first time in my life I think I understand religion.'

'I see,' she said.

'What do you mean, you see.'

There was a pause on the line and Tom used it to quietly fish out another cigarette from the pack. He placed it between his lips and spoke around it. 'What do you mean?'

'Tom, I'm a Christian.'

'What?' The cigarette tumbled from his mouth and he rushed to put out the fire, then realized it was unlit.

'Obviously, I haven't been a very good one.'

'Listen,' he said gripping the phone as if he were afraid it would morph into something bizarre if he didn't hold on tightly. 'I'm going to call Dr. Wackes back. Would you go back with me to talk to him?'

'Of course. I'll get off work around 5:00.'

That evening, after Tom and Linda left Dr. Wackes' office, they went out to dinner.

'Do you feel any different?' Linda asked glancing at him with cautious eyes as if this were a first date and not her husband of several years.

'You know,' she continued, 'Tonight in his office, Dr. Wackes said if anyone comes to Christ he becomes a new creation – a new person. I was just wondering if you felt any different since you asked Jesus in your heart.'

Tom sat for a moment and stared at the pack of cigarettes. He had been absently flipping them end over end. 'It's funny you ask that,' he said, not taking his eyes from the little box he continued to rotate. 'The sight of these cigarettes fills me with nausea. I've chain-smoked for the past months, but I have zero desire to have one now.'

'Uh,' Linda said, choking on her drink. She slammed her water down and coughed several times.

Tom patted her back as she gasped for air. He laughed in spite of her distress because of the incredulous grin on her face.

It surprised Tom, but he got the job at Westminster Academy. He met weekly with some of the teachers who mentored him in his new Christian faith.

Dr. Kennedy held a seminar that fall with Dr. Gish and Dr. Morris, the fathers of the creation movement. Tom attended. He spent most of the weekend listening in open-mouthed disbelief.

He told Linda later, 'I've never heard anyone speak so logically and profoundly about Creation.' He smacked the sofa with his fist and frowned with frustration. 'I've been so deceived. This is monumental. I have got to know more.'

He bought every book offered at the seminar and pored over them relearning science from a Biblical standpoint. *It took more faith for me to believe the crazy things about evolution than this,* he thought. *This just makes sense. How could I have been so blind?*

Not only did he teach creation science to the students at Westminster Academy, but he also began teaching a class during the Sunday school hour at Coral Ridge. He even worked some of it into the curriculum at the public junior college where he taught in the summers.

Dr. Kennedy recognized Tom's gift for teaching and encouraged him in his studies. Creation science was also one of Jim's passions. He preached that evolution was one of Satan's deadliest tools. 'Every single anti-Christian system that dominates our world rests its case on evolution. Two massive non-Christian movements today are: in the East, Communism and the West, secular humanism. Both of these atheistic systems rest upon the single pillar of evolution.'

For years Tom felt as if he had stumbled blindly down the path of life, unsure where he was going. After he trusted Christ, learned the trustworthiness of Scripture, and saw the facts of creationism fulfilled scientifically, he knew where he wanted to go. He met with Dr. Kennedy one afternoon and confided in him.

'Dr. Kennedy, you have pioneered the trail and paved the way for me to follow.'

Jim sat forward, rested his elbows on his desk and steepled his fingers. He smiled, but a furrow knitted his brow as if unsure where Tom was heading. 'How is that?'

'When I first became a Christian and joined the church, you preached a series of sermons on creation and evolution. It rocked my world. I had never heard anyone speak so eloquently and with such conviction. I know you've preached Creationism since the seventies.'

'Sixties,' Jim corrected with a wink.

'I bet there aren't many preachers who have done that.'

'I'm not a betting man,' Jim said in a teasing voice, 'but I'd say you are probably right.'

'You know I have become a diligent student of creation science.' It was a statement, not a question and Jim nodded.

'God has laid something on my heart and I think you'll be interested.'

'Shoot.'

'I want to form an organization – Citizens for Scientific Integrity – not only to teach students, but also laymen, about creationism. I want to take people on field trips so they can learn tactilely. We will dig up dinosaur bones and view strata of layers in canyon walls that point to Noah's flood. We will do radio programs and write articles. I would even like to open a museum to exhibit our findings.'

Jim inched forward as Tom spoke. The wrinkles on his face deepened as his smile and his eyes widened. 'I love it. That's a great idea.' He reached across the desk to grasp Tom's hand.

I have a high regard for people with vision. We don't have a lot of money for another project right now, but I will back you any way I can.'

Jim Kennedy did what he said. He not only preached creationism from the pulpit, he supported the new ministry giving Tom space to run it and everything he needed to advance.

During the 90's Tom piloted the Creation Studies Institute, CSI. Westminster Academy not only governed the ministry, it gave Tom latitude when more of his time was taken from teaching as the institute developed. Among other accomplishments, parts of three different mammoths were excavated on field trips CSI took with the school.

Around 2002 Coral Ridge Ministries elected to take over the governing of CSI. It had outgrown its facilities and needed more funding from the church. Tom hugged Linda. 'I have never been happier. I am in my dream job.'

Linda laughed. 'Remember when you wanted to work with AT & T?'

'Thank God, He doesn't always give us what we think we want.'

'But He has given you the desires of your heart.'

'Yes, I could not ask for anything more.' Tom stood up then exhaled with a sigh. 'I am not feeling so great,' he said and sat back down.

'Tom? What's wrong?' Linda clutched his arm.

'I am not sure. Lately, I have been feeling a bit weak.' He slumped in the chair.

'You look pale. I think we ought to get you to a doctor.'

That afternoon they received an unanticipated diagnosis. In the midst of the excitement of building CSI, disease had silently attacked Tom. His family reacted with shock when they discovered there was nothing they could do to help him. He needed a kidney transplant in order to survive, but none of his kin matched, not even his sister.

Eighty-five thousand people throughout the nation were waiting for transplants, but only about six thousand kidneys are donated each year. An average of sixteen Americans die each day waiting for a kidney transplant.

Death of a dream. Death of a man on the threshold of such great things. Lost, lost echoed in the corridors of his mind, but Tom refused to listen. He fixed his trust in the Lord and refused to despair.

Many of the church members wrote or called with condolences. Tom wasn't surprised to get several calls from one of the church deacons, Joe Pettit. Tom barely knew Joe but was touched by the younger man's compassion. Joe suggested the church sponsor a blood drive for him. Perhaps some members might sign up for a possible transplant. 'Maybe we could get a donor out of the deal,' he told Tom over the phone.

'Sure,' Tom said, trying to sound upbeat. 'Sounds good.'

Two weeks later Joe received a call from the testing coordinator at the hospital.

'Yes,' he said into the phone. 'Really?' his voice rose an octave higher than usual. 'Me?' He paused. 'Are you sure?'

That evening Joe talked to his family over dinner. 'What would you think if I donated one of my kidneys to Tom DeRosa?'

Clank! His wife dropped her fork onto her plate and began to cough.

'Who?' his younger daughter asked, 'is Tom DeRosa?'

His older daughter thumped her sister in the arm. 'You know, he's the dinosaur guy at school.'

His wife caught her breath and spluttered. 'Are you serious?'

'Daddy, that is so cool. It is like Jesus, sort of. You know,' she gestured at him with a fork full of beans. 'You know, that verse we learned in Sunday school, "Whoever has the most love gives his life for somebody or something like that."'

'Daddy,' his younger daughter shrieked, 'you're going to die?'

'Joe! You hardly know Tom DeRosa. Are you sure you want to give him your kidney?'

'What is a kidney? Is it in your brain?'

Tom held his hands up to stop the machine-gun chatter. 'Wait! Stop! Let me answer your questions one at a time.' He turned to his younger daughter. 'We all have two kidneys. If I give one away I will still be okay.'

'Unless something happens to your other one,' his older daughter said with superiority.

He turned to his wife. 'I realize I hardly know Tom, but the Lord has laid him on my heart. I have been praying about it and searching the Scripture for guidance. The words of Psalm 139 keep coming into my mind. "In Thy book all my days were written down even before there was one of them." My life is in God's hands. He knows when I will die. Whether it is on the freeway or on the operating table, my times are in His hands.'

His wife hugged him. 'I'm so glad I've married a godly man who considers others above himself.'

Dr. Gaetano Ciancio, the University of Miami's Medical Center professor of surgery and urology, thought Joe Pettit might be a good candidate for their psych ward. He suggested Joe see psychologists before undergoing the surgery. Joe thought the doctor was trying to talk him out of donating his kidney. 'Are you really, really, really sure?' Dr. Ciancio kept asking him. 'You are a healthy man. You don't have to do this.'

When he was finally convinced Joe meant business and he was not crazy, the doctor's paradigm shifted. 'Joe,' he said with reverence in his voice, 'you are a hero.'

'No, doctor, don't say that. I am no hero. The Lord has led me to do this, every step of the way.'

Dr. Ciancio shook his head and asked himself. *'Would I do this?'* He shook his head thoughtfully. *'I don't know.'*

The surgery was a great success. Because of Joe's gift of life, Tom was able to continue his vision to reach people for Christ through the Creation Studies Institute. Through CRI's website, radio program, lectures, field trips and new museum they educate thousands on the truth of God's creation.

33

26.2 AND COUNTING

'This is 911. Is there a problem?'

'Yes, my house is on fire,' Jennifer Kennedy said in a cool voice.

'Stay on the line. We'll have someone there right away. Are you in a safe place?'

'Yes, I came to a neighbor's house.'

'Just stay calm.'

'I am calm.'

'Is there anyone else in the house?'

'No, I live with my parents, but they are out of town.'

'How did the fire start?'

'The icemaker in the fridge leaked and soaked the carpet in the living room. A neighbor set up fans to dry out the rugs. One of them caught on fire.'

As soon as Jennifer left the neighbor's a man pulled into her driveway and jumped out of his car. He grabbed something out of the back seat then ran up and kicked in the front door!

Smoke billowed around the stranger and obscured him from Jennifer's view, but she heard a hissing, kwahh, kwahh, kwahh, and recognized the noise as that of a fire extinguisher.

Moments later, Jennifer heard the wail of a siren and a fire truck roared into the quiet neighborhood, its swirling lights streaming into the dark corners. Jennifer checked her watch, 4:15 a.m. It had taken the firemen fifteen minutes to get there. In that time this mystery man had saved her parents house from total destruction.

'A plainclothes policeman,' she said in surprise after he introduced himself. 'Thanks for going above and beyond your call of duty.'

'I was in the neighborhood and heard the distress signal on the radio. The night was slow and I had this with me.' He patted the empty extinguisher. 'Thought I wouldd come join the fun.'

Although the house did not burn to the ground, the air conditioner had sucked the burning plastic into the vents and distributed toxic gunk throughout the house coating the carpet, beds and furniture. Virtually everything had to be replaced.

Jim shook his head when he heard the news. 'You know what this means, Anne?' he asked.

'What?'

'You know I've been tithing one hundred percent of our salary.'

'Yes, I know.'

'It's going to be very expensive to rebuild and replace everything the fire destroyed.'

'That's true.'

'I guess we should view this as a sign from God. Maybe we ought to rethink our giving.'

Anne stiffened. 'But God has always met our needs, Jim. The more you give away, the more he gives back.'

'Yes, that's true. That is why I think we should rethink our giving.'

Anne raised her hands. 'It's up to you, Jim. But I don't think backing down our giving is a good idea.'

'I agree. But since we will need to replace everything and it will be expensive, I think we should increase our giving again.'

'How can you increase more than one hundred percent?'

'I want to tithe all the honorariums I get for speaking engagements, all gifts people give us, and any royalties I get for books I have written. We can continue giving one hundred percent of my salary plus twenty-five percent of all other income that comes our way. It will be fun to see how God will meet our needs through this accident.'

Anne laughed. 'I can't argue with you. I told you long ago I'd follow where God leads. He's never let us down. I'll continue to trust Him to guide you and to meet our needs.'

Two years after the fire ravaged their home, Jennifer began training for a marathon. Anne grabbed her one morning before her run and said, 'Jennifer, can we talk a minute?'

'Sure, Mom. What's up?'

'Your dad and I love having you here with us. You know that don't you?'

'Do you want me to leave?'

'No, don't be silly. Your dad and I are just worried about your relationship with Chip.'

'I know, Mom. Eight years is a long time to date.'

'Don't you think it's time to move on? He must not be serious enough to marry you, and you are wasting your tender years on him.'

'You think I am not going to be an eligible bachelorette if I keep dating him indefinitely.'

'That's not the only reason. Eight years is long enough to date someone if they won't commit. We don't want to see you hurt. Maybe it's time to move on.'

'I agree, Mom. I can't keep holding on, but I don't want to think about it till after this marathon. It takes all my effort just to train. I just can't think about this right now.'

'If it wears you out so bad, maybe you shouldn't do it.'

'Oh, Mom! I ran track in high school, played tennis, basketball and every other sport under the sun. I'm in shape. It is just that 26.2 miles is a long way. I have always wanted to run a marathon. This will be fun in a twisted sort of way. Besides, it is in Disney World. If I get tired I can hitch a ride on Dumbo or something.'

A month later Jennifer crossed the finish line in the Magic Kingdom in five hours twenty minutes. Chip waited at the finish line with a dozen red roses.

'Hey,' Jennifer asked. 'What are you doing here.' She was surprised to see him since he had been sick with the flu all week.

'How could I not come? This is your big day. I am proud of you and want to support you. If you get sick now it won't hinder your race time.'

'I still don't want to catch your bug. I can't believe you dragged yourself out of bed to come see me finish. You are terrific.' Jennifer smelled the roses and smiled up at him over their petals.

She noticed Chip had a polo shirt on over a T-shirt, but didn't think much of it since it was a little cool and he was sick. But the next thing she knew he had grabbed the tail of it and pulled it over his head. Squaring his shoulders as if Jennifer had shouted, 'Atten hut!' Chip stood straight in front of her. However, his grin was so wide, no true drill sergeant would have approved.

'What –,' Jennifer started then stopped when she noticed the writing on Chip's T-shirt.

It was slightly crumpled. She looked at it closely and read the words aloud, 'Hey blondie. Will you marry me?'

Chip turned around and she saw that the back of his shirt was printed with several lines. She grabbed it with both hands to pull the material straight and began to read aloud.

'"1991 – 'The first'"'

'Remember?' Chip asked as he looked over his shoulder.

Jennifer laughed. 'Our first date! The Miami vs. FSU game. How could I ever forget?' She ran her finger down the list to the next item underneath 1991.

'"1992 – Jennifer turns thirty." You totally decorated my yard with signs, banners and balloons. I was so embarrassed.'

'Keep reading,' Chip said.

'1993 – Notre Dame vs. Boston College – South Bend.'

'1994 – Almost traded girlfriend for Notre Dame vs. FSU ticket'

'You laughed! I remember.'

'When you meet your boyfriend's best friend at a football game, and your boyfriend makes a sign saying he'll trade you for game tickets, what can a girl do but laugh.'

'That's what I love about you. You can laugh at anything.'

'"1995 C.E. Cassidy, Inc." You finally started your own business.'

Chip nodded.

'"1996 – Jenn becomes a real nurse – Lake Wawasee summer." I always was a real nurse. Just because I worked in administrative positions didn't mean I wasn't a nurse.'

'I loved going with you to Indiana. Lake Wawasee was an amazing trip,' Chip said and tried to turn around. Jennifer held him in place.

'Hold still, I haven't finished reading yet.'

'Yes, Ma'am.'

'I am going to enjoy this moment. I have waited a long time for it. Stop shaking. I can't read with you laughing.'

'"1997 Key Largo by Wawasee." Your sister's boat, the Wawasee.' Jennifer almost whispered the last words. 'That was a great trip to the Keys.'

'"1998 – The Fire." She shuddered. 'I hope I never have to flee a burning house again.'

'1999 – Chip turns 40.'

'2000 – 8 years and 26.2 miles later. Forever....'

Chip turned around slowly and caressed Jennifer's face with his hands. 'Now that you've finished your marathon, will you marry me and be with me forever?'

She wrapped her arms around him and buried her face on his shoulder.

'I guess this means yes?' Chip said, his voice rising at the end in a question mark as he slid the ring on her finger.

Jennifer just nodded. He stroked her hair and kissed the top of her head. He hugged her for a moment then held her at arm's length. 'What do you think your folks will say?'

'It's about time,' Jennifer said with an imitation of her dad's low voice.

34

THE GREAT ADVENTURE

Forty-five years. On May 22, 1960, eleven months after Jim and Anne moved to Fort Lauderdale to plant a new church, Coral Ridge Presbyterian achieved official status as a church. In 2005 a celebration was held to commemorate forty-five years of successful service for Christ. The church stands, not only as a towering edifice, but a lighthouse for heaven. The ministries spawned from it have not only impacted Fort Lauderdale, Florida, but the world.

From Afghanistan – 'I want to first thank you for your generosity in supplying the books and videos that greatly assisted in the facilitation of our ministry. Nothing prepared us for the response we had for the DVD [*Who Is This Jesus?*]. I have had dozens of requests for it. If you could provide more, it would be greatly appreciated. Please let me know. Thank you again for your time. God Bless!'

From Syria – 'Thank God for this amazing grace to be able to contact you in the U.S. from Syria through the Internet. You have here a great reputation in our churches because of your ministry programs, especially the broadcast programs.'

From Iraq – 'I am currently serving with the U.S. Army here in Iraq. Morale is high and we hope that the constant drumbeat of "bad news" back there in the States will not impact our ability to finish the job we have come to do. So much "good news" goes unreported or under-reported.

'Thank you for your stalwart support of the values that built our great nation. I ask that you would hold our troops and our precious families in prayer. Our families pay a tremendous price in sacrificing for the freedom we enjoy. They are true heroes and deserve our support.'

The ministries created by Jim Kennedy have influenced count-less people around the world.

Evangelism Explosion is in 230 nations and territories around the globe. It has trained pastors and lay people to share their faith in their own tongue, tribes and nations. In the first five years of the 21st Century E.E. trained people in every nation on earth and led 25 million people to Christ. To God be the glory!

Westminster Academy has educated and trained 2,615 students to be movers and shakers in their world for Christ.

CRM's radio ministry is heard in 202 countries.

The television ministry reaches 40,000 cities in America and 165 countries.

Knox Theological Seminary has seen 787 men and women study in their halls.

The Center for Christian Statesmanship has been in operation for ten years reaching and affecting the Nation's leaders for righteousness.

The Center for Reclaiming America showed its mettle as Christians made their presence known in recent elections.

The Creation Studies Institute has educated thousands across America through workshops, conferences, newsletters and their Fort Lauderdale museum.

After 45 years of ministering Dr. D. James Kennedy continues to reach the world for Christ. He has authored sixty-seven books. Many of these have been translated into foreign languages. In spite of constant pain from his childhood football injury and other painful conditions he stands in the pulpit each Sunday to preach the Word of God.

The year 2005 was disastrous for the southern coastal cities in America. After deadly hurricanes trounced New Orleans and Texas, another supposed smaller one approached the coast of Fort Lauderdale. As Hurricane Wilma approached land the category five storm was downgraded by the National Weather Forecast to a level one.

'We've been through several category one hurricanes,' Jim told Jennifer when she wanted to stay and help her parents weather the storm.

'I know, Dad, but you never know. I'll come just in case.'

The Kennedy household slept peacefully throughout the winds and rain. But the next morning when Jennifer and her dad went to check on the church, they were shocked. The disc jockey on the car radio was just saying, 'It's been the worst storm to hit us in fifty years,' when they drove in front of the church.

'We can't even pull into the parking lot,' Jennifer said in a flat hushed voice. 'Oh, its terrible. All those beautiful ficus trees.'

'There's a spiritual lesson in this,' Jim said, 'Those trees were tall and stately, but they had shallow roots. Many Christians appear strong and righteous, but when the storms of life hit, they topple because their walk with God and depth in His Word are shallow.'

Jennifer glanced sideways. 'Oh, Dad. I don't want this to upset you.'

'When have you seen anything bother me?' he asked. 'I learned long ago that God always provides. How can I worry? He is in control. He is the Lord of the Dance, and it's amazing to watch and see what steps He takes.'

'How much are you giving now?' Jennifer asked. 'I know you gave 200 percent last year. Weren't you scared?'

Jim grinned and shrugged his shoulders. 'It was a little scary, but in an exciting way. We have learned that you can't out-give God.' He squeezed her hand with his left and threw his right, palm up, to the sky. 'It was fun too. I love living by the hand of God.'

As they entered the sanctuary, Jennifer reached down to turn up her pant legs. 'I can't believe there's this much water on the floor.'

Jim looked up and squinted. Light streamed in shafts through the gaps torn in the roof. He grimaced.

Jennifer noticed and said, 'Dad, I don't want this to hurt your heart.'

He put an arm around her. 'This is just another opportunity to do what my seminary professor told me to do so long ago.'

'What's that?'

'Stand still and see the salvation of God.'

'Excuse me, Dr. Kennedy?' an assistant pastor called Jim from the door of the sanctuary. 'I was in the parking lot when a truck drove by. It wheeled around and the driver asked if we needed any help. I think you should come and talk to him.'

Jim and Jennifer climbed over the fallen trees and stepped around debris that littered every inch of the parking lot. A tall, thin man leaned against a large white pickup which had parked awkwardly on the sidewalk. As he stepped away from the truck to shake hands, Jim saw a magnetic sign plastered on the driver's door.

'Statewide Disaster Relief Company,' Jim read aloud.

'Yes, sir. We followed the hurricane down here. Figured it may be worse than predicted. We can have this cleared up in a matter of days.'

Jim looked over his shoulder at the wreckage behind him. 'A few days. You've got to be kidding. This looks like it will take weeks. Or months.'

The disaster relief man grinned. 'You'll be surprised. We'll have our machines here by tomorrow and you'll be singing hymns by Sunday.'

Five days later a courageous crowd gathered to worship. The cleanup had been such a success, no one could believe how bad it had been till they watched a video that displayed the destruction. As usual, the CRM team did a first-rate job in putting the short film together complete with the financial breakdown of the repair cost. On a tall screen behind the podium, images of fallen trees, sodden carpet, and structural damage flashed and a smooth professional voice told the damage. 'Insurance will cover most everything,' it said. 'However, our deductible is a quarter of a million dollars.'

An audible gasp chorused from the congregation.

Sunday afternoon, when Jim and Anne got back home, Jim grabbed Anne's hand. 'Guess what?' he said with eyes that twinkled like a kid's at Christmas.

'What?' Anne asked.

'I love being in the ministry!'

'Me too,' she agreed.

'It is so fun to watch God provide.'

'What happened?'

'One of the prominent businessmen in our congregation came to me after the service and said, "Dr. Kennedy, the check is in the mail."'

'The check. What check?'

'The check for a quarter of a million dollars.'

'The insurance deductible!' Anne said with a happy squeak in her voice.

'Isn't God good?'

'To dance with Him is a great adventure!'

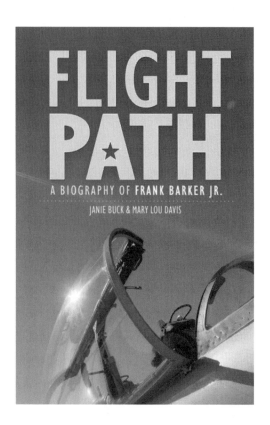

FLIGHT
PATH

A BIOGRAPHY OF FRANK BARKER JR.

JANIE BUCK & MARY LOU DAVIS

Flight Path

A Biography of Frank Barker Jr

Janie Buck & Mary Lou Davis

'I do not believe that anyone can read this exciting and moving story of lives lived for the kingdom of God without becoming a better person through the experience.'

D. James Kennedy,
Coral Ridge Presbyterian Church, Fort Lauderdale, Florida

'I highly recommend this book to young pastors because it will enrich their ministry. They will discover the central ingredients of the Christian life and how to have a missions program that will be a blessing to the entire world. I thank God for Frank Barker.'

The Late Bill Bright,
Founder and Chairman of Campus Crusade for Christ Intl.

'This is the page-turning story of one of the most remarkable ministers of the Gospel I have ever known. I wish that every young minister could spend a year under the tutelage of Frank Barker. A great read about a mighty man of God!'

Timothy George,
Dean, Beeson Divinity School, Birmingham, Alabama

'The story of Frank Barker is an amazing account of how God uses the faithful and the humble. In a marvelous way Christ sought him, saved him, and made him an effective instrument for the building up of the church. What a remarkable and encouraging legacy!'

John MacArthur,
Grace Community Church, Los Angeles, California

ISBN 1-85792-918-7